Aristotle in a New Perspective

Introduction to the Theory of the Four Discourses

Olavo de Carvalho

Translated by
Anthony Doyle

ASHMAN
FREE PRESS

To request permissions, contact the publisher at danielashman@protonmail.com.

ISBN: 978-1-7360306-6-0 (Paperback)
ISBN: 978-1-7360306-5-3 (eBook)

First paperback edition November 2022.

Translated by Anthony Doyle
Indexed by Michael Hendry
Back cover photo credit by Mauro Ventura
Creative Director Brian Giles

Key Producers
Pedro de Carvalho
Mariana Reis Dean

ASHMAN FREE PRESS
Boston, MA

ASHMANFREEPRESS.COM

I dedicate this book to my mother
Nicéa Pimentel de Carvalho

and to the memory of my father
Luiz Gonzaga de Carvalho

"*The greater the work accomplished (and greatness is in no way equivalent to the extent and number of writings) the richer the unthought-of element in that work. That is, the richer is that which, through this work and through it alone, comes toward us as never yet thought of.*"

- MARTIN HEIDEGGER

Contents

Aristotle at the Dentist: A Polemic Between the Author and the SPBC

Prologue

T HIS BOOK IS OLD AND NEW. It includes *An Aristotelian Philosophy of Culture*, originally published in 1994, plus four new chapters (The Universal Typology of the Discourses;[1] Reasons for Credibility; Milestones in the History of Aristotelian Studies; and Notes for a Possible Conclusion), and a supplement titled "Aristotle at the Dentist: Polemic between the Author and the Sociedade Brasileira para o Progresso de Ciência—SBPC (Brazilian Society for the Advancement of Science)".[2] The added chapters are not exactly new, though they are previously unpublished, having circulated thus far only as booklets used on my courses. For its part, the supplement, in circulation for a time as a brochure annexed to some copies of *An Aristotelian Philosophy of Culture,* contains: (a) my response to the Editorial Committee of the journal *Ciência Hoje* regarding its outlandish "Critical Assessment" of my *An Aristotelian Philosophy of Culture*; (b) an article I published in *O Globo* newspaper in response to two windbags who, talking through their tasseled mortarboard hats, came out in defense of the indefensible and decided to sound off against a thesis they admitted to not having actually read (perhaps it was a case of critical telepathy, I can't say); and (c) some letters I sent to the director of the publication, Ênio Candotti, trying my best to remind him of his duties, an effort he resisted so valiantly that I finally understood what the old theology meant by the expression *ignorantia invincibilis*.

In the volley of polemics sparked by *An Aristotelian Philosophy of Culture* between December 1994 and February 1995 in the Rio de Janeiro press, the most intriguing aspect was that my opponents, prodigious in forming opinions about the character of an author they had never even met, not on that or any other day's walk, seemed incapable of saying a single word about the content of the thesis in question, which, having nothing whatsoever to do with the usual gossip-mongering of the city's bored old crabs, was as beyond their range of comprehension as it was their sphere of interests. When publicly challenged to discuss said thesis, they preferred to run for the arrowslits of personal insult, behind which their trembling, rancorous souls felt so much more at home, perhaps for its being their natural habitat. It so happened that, by (un)lucky coincidence, while this particular brouhaha was unfolding in *O Globo*, another, concerning something entirely unrelated, was playing out in the pages of *O Jornal do Brasil*, and the two controversies ended up becoming one. Naturally, this would never have happened had certain supposedly intellectualized noggins of our nation not seen matters less in accordance with the categorical distinctions of Aristotle than with a puerile Eisensteinian collision montage or a "logic of appearances" in Epicurean molds, a method in which your average swine or fowl can attain a certain proficiency before even reaching maturity. And as the subject of this second controversy was nothing less explosive than the moral judgment of the intelligentsia, which, rightly or wrongly, I was accusing of unconscious complicity with Rio's banditry,[3] it happens that certain members of the class, feeling scratched somewhere sensitive on their collective epidermis, yet not quite sure from which direction the offending briar had been swung, decided that it was probably prudent to aim their retaliations at my innocent Aristotle as well, just in case. And to do that, naturally, it was far better not to have read the thing. The result was an imbroglio of the maddest sort, in which a guilty conscience, class vanities, ideological grouse, a prodigious dearth of philosophical culture and a firm resolution not to understand a thing joined forces to ensure a united battle charge could be launched against something they had not the foggiest idea what, but from which their collective olfactory cells, thrumming like those of a yokel in New York, believed they had detected the vague scent of danger. Watching those skittish little ducklings rush for the protective wing of collegial solidarity, I could not help but wonder whether, in the little play they were staging in their minds, I had not been cast in the role of the fox in the chicken coop. Flattering indeed, I would say, given my diminutive stature, but also utterly nuts. Or perhaps not: perhaps theirs was a precise foreboding that a voice raised in all seriousness, with the kind of sincerity that unites heart and mind, ethos and logos, could truly spoil the effect of the meticulously woven comedy which Brazilian intellectual life had become, waking up the public and forcing the troupe of hackneyed clowns to find a new line of work. I don't know, and I really don't care; it's their problem.

My problem, the only one that concerned me, was to know whether or not there was an overriding unity to the four discourses in Aristotle's logic, and if it might yield anything useful to our present search for an interdisciplinary knowledge. I can't for the life of me understand how those ninnies could possibly have imagined that a guy up to his neck in a thorny question like that would have the time or the inclination to care what they happened to think of his good person, a subject he barely addresses himself, having long since shaken off the egocentric conflicts of adolescence and discovered the existence of a vast and wonderful world out there beyond the outer rim of his own bellybutton. Nor do I entertain the slightest curiosity as to their characters, because their conduct, however stupid it might be, hardly provides sufficient elements on which to judge their respective personalities, *terra incognita* to me and not, in the strictest sense of the word, an issue. Forming opinions about one's peers is one of the most wasteful occupations a man can find for his measly life. As the saying goes: *Masters talk about things, servants, about people.*

Chapter V, which reproduces a lecture I gave at the

Philosophy Seminary, will help the reader grasp the historical perspective in which, within the wider evolution of Aristotelian studies, my investigation on the Four Discourses so deliberately inserts itself; and that perspective, once caught at least in passing, will give some measure of how vitally important the theme of this book is not only to the History of Philosophy, but also to the conception of a global and integrated culture, indeed a global and integrated education, in which the brightest hopes for humanity find themselves deposited today. The contrast between the elevated nature of these cogitations and the pettiness of the reactions my book incited in certain circles does not stoke in me any pangs of revolt, as my sinful soul is far more inclined to gluttony, sloth and lust than to fits of wrath, but it does cause a certain irremediable sadness, one laced with somber forebodings as to the role Brazil intends to play in the spiritual history of the world. It's a sadness I disguise behind laughter—the melancholic laughter of a spectator forced to endure a historical tragicomedy.

One way or another, reproducing these documents in the present volume does not merely serve to record for posterity a lamentable reality of the present. My response to the SBPC "consultant" contains some important developments to the core argument, including a metaphysical perspective intentionally omitted from the main body of the work. Whatever demerits said individual might have, I cannot deny that I was at least given occasion to provide explanations that, awaiting opportunity for still more detailed developments, I may not otherwise have had the chance to proffer.[4]

It is also important to add that not everyone in the Brazilian university milieu imitates the kind of thinking done by those three neurons that, at the last count, occupy the skull of the director of *Ciência Hoje*, and which, one presumes out of frugality, he shares with Professors Gilberto Velho and Carlos Henrique Escobar, leaving none whatsoever for Mr. Antônio Callado (who, alas, once had them in abundance, but used them all up penning the novel *Quarup*). Writing on the episode in a letter published in *O Globo* newspaper at the time, Fernando de Mello Gomide made some pertinent observations about the philosophical unculture of our scientific elites. And soon after that, the Catholic University of Salvador, state of Bahia, in the person of the academic coordinator of the Institute of Philosophy and the Humanities, Prof. Dante Augusto Galeffi, took the initiative of restoring the honor of Brazil's university community by inviting me to deliver a series of lectures on the book's theme throughout May 1995 (under the title I later adopted for the present volume). Thankfully, I was able to address an audience of the most intelligent and diligent minds I have ever encountered among Brazilian students. In the end, the stain tarnishing the reputation of our academic establishment was finally removed by Prof. Miguel Reale, who accepted an abbreviated version of this work for the Fifth Brazilian Philosophy Conference held in São Paulo in September 1995, and at which I finally had the opportunity to hear and address worthy and intelligent objections presented by three genuine men of knowledge: Milton Vargas, Romano Galeffi and Gaston Duval.

I cannot fail to thank all of those who supported me in

this battle, which I neither sought nor fled from, against establishment ignorance. Evandro Carlos de Andrade opened the pages of *O Globo* to me so that I could mount my defense, making the fight between this illustrious unknown scholar and the conclave of cardinals gathered under the apostolic blessing of Pope Ennius I a little less unfair. Elizabeth Orsini wrote an excellent article that brought the debacle to wider public attention. Bruno Tolentino, with that rich satirical vein he inherited from his forebear Nicolau, waded in on my side and turned the big-wigs at the SBPC into a national laughingstock. And, among all those who wrote to me, or in my defense in the Rio press, the philologist Daniel Brilhante de Brito deserves special mention. Some weeks after the whole thing blew up, I sent a copy of *An Aristotelian Philosophy of Culture* to the respected Hellenist, asking him to subject my discussions of Aristotle's vocabulary to rigorous inspection. I did this quaking in my boots, fearing it would transpire that I knew about as much Greek as the SBPC "assessor" did philosophy. I alone can know the relief I felt when, rather than take me aside for a dressing down, the master wrote to the *Jornal do Brasil* to praise me in public, and just when the philosophagites were about to roast me alive.

Needless to say, the whole SBPC episode marked me deeply, showing that the ineptness of our intelligentsia runs far deeper and wider than the odd display that had reached my antennae until then. The impact of the experience was depressing at first, much like a teacher who spends months giving her very best to instruct her class on a particular topic only to discover that they haven't understood a thing. This realization that all that pedagogic effort has come to nothing would, as was certainly my case, trigger a terrible loneliness, the sense of being alone in a strange land, surrounded by strangers. It reminded me of the *Dialogue of the Conversion of the Heathen*, in which Fr. Manoel da Nóbrega, after describing his initial joy at converting his first Amerindians, was later dismayed to see that his converts had taken the faith purely for the sake of it and had not actually absorbed the meaning of a single teaching by which they had supposedly been Christianized. I could imagine the solitude this missionary must have felt, thousands of miles away from home, upon realizing that he had been talking to the four walls all along—or, for lack of walls in the New World, to the coconut trees and the armadillos. That was precisely what I felt in the face of the SBPC: intellectual life in Brazil was a shell with absolutely nothing living inside, and there was I, a complete idiot, thinking all along that I had been dialoguing with sentient creatures. It was then, in a shadowy and shapeless form, that first arose the inspiration for the book *The Collective Imbecile*, intended as a sort of defibrillator to revive the moribund patient. So when, today, I hear those same creatures proclaim that I wrote the book merely to draw attention to myself, I see that they have drifted even further from reality than the SBPC debacle had made me think. It never even crosses their minds that I might have written that book to draw attention to *them*.

Prologue

So by republishing the pacific speculations that gave rise to so much combat, and by contemplating the furious driveling of those poor fellows who insist on denying me the title of philosopher just so they can retain the illusion that they ever had the power to grant it, I keep alive inside myself the irony of the situation. I'm reminded of the scene from that Woody Allen film in which Zelig, the "hero without any character",[5] locked up in a mental institution, receives his daily visit from his psychiatrist utterly convinced that he's the therapist and she, his patient. Hardly coincidentally, in his own imaginary university, Zelig held the chair in masturbation.

Rio de Janeiro, September 1996

A Preliminary Note to the First Edition of An Aristotelian Philosophy of Culture

THE FIRST OF THE TEXTS that comprise this book has been circulating in hand-out form since 1993, and the second, since 1992. They summarize an idea I have been presenting in my courses since 1987, namely that Aristotle's Poetics, Rhetoric, Dialectic and Logic (Analytics), all founded upon common principles, form a single science.

When presenting itself in book form, however slim and modest, the least one would expect of an opinion so contrary to the prevailing interpretations of a major philosopher's work, not just today, but down through the centuries, is that it should offer itself up to scrutiny in the most complete, precise and extensively demonstrable manner possible—clearly not the case with the present volume. Here, the idea is laid out in compact form, shored by only some general indications of the most promising lines of possible demonstration.[1]

Not that the idea itself is merely a seed silently warming in the author's mind: its complete and robust elucidation and defense have been made on numerous occasions in my courses, as recorded on tape and transcribed in hand-outs.[2] An unusually busy life that in no way resembles the peaceful routine of a scholar among tomes, as the theme of this work might reasonably suggest to the reader, has prevented me from giving the present material an adequate and definitive written format. As that reality is unlikely to change any time soon, I decided, in light of the unfeasibility of a more elaborate treatment, to at least present a provisory sketch of my interpretation of Aristotle, lest some smart aleck—the sort that makes up a good quarter or third of our men and women of letters—should, having heard me propose it in my courses and lectures, or perhaps reproduced by someone who had, decide to present it as their own original discovery.

Because discover it I did. More than that: I devoted some long years of my life to it, lending it such ample practical applications in the fields of pedagogy and philosophical methodology that I dare to think the Stagirite master himself would not have altogether disapproved. And so, whilst I cannot spend sufficient time licking the cub, nor will I simply hand it over to the first passing wolf.

Hence, as a mere precaution, I decided to publish this outline, which, however brief and unsatisfactory, does not, I believe, suffer from any fatal imprecision or serious shortcoming, but rather serves as a worthy enough introduction to further and more complete expositions that may still, God willing, see light of day.

Rio de Janeiro, August 1994

1. The Four Discourses

THERE IS A CORE IDEA embedded in the works of Aristotle, and it has escaped the attention of almost all his readers and commentators from Antiquity to the present day. Even those who have grasped it down through the millennia—I know of only two—merely noted it in passing, without explicitly affording it any decisive importance with regard to a comprehensive understanding of Aristotle's philosophy.[1] And yet, it is the very key to such an understanding, if by that we mean the act of capturing the unity of a man's thought right from his own intentions and values, rather than judging it from the outside in; an act that implies carefully respecting what is written between the lines, as it were, instead of smothering the work under some wrongheaded idolatry of the reified text, the very tomb of thought.

I call it the *Theory of the Four Discourses*, and it can basically be summed up as follows: human discourse is a single power that manifests in four distinct ways: poetics, rhetoric, dialectic, and analytics (logic).

Put so simply, it doesn't seem such a groundbreaking idea. But, if we recall that the names attributed to those four modalities of discourse are also the designations of four sciences, we see that it therefore follows that Poetics, Rhetoric, Dialectics and Logic, approached as modalities of a single power, are also, by extension, *variants of one and the same science*. This diversification into four subordinate sciences must, lest we break the Aristotelian rule of divisions, rest upon the unicity of their common subject. And that means that the principles of each presuppose the existence of common principles under which all four are subsumed; principles, that is, that apply equally to such disparate fields as scientific demonstration and the construction of a tragic plot in drama. Seen in this light, the apparently simple idea I floated about Aristotle's philosophy begins to look rather strange, surprising, even extravagant. And it suggests, straight off, two key questions: first, is that what Aristotle really thought? And, if so, was he right? Addressing these questions entails a twofold approach: a historical/philological investigation, on one hand, and a philosophical critique, on the other. I do neither satisfactorily within the scope of the present work, and merely inquire as to the reasons for all the puzzlement.

The perplexity which the idea of the Four Discourses provokes at first sight stems from our culture's deeply ingrained habit of assigning poetic language and logical or scientific language to distinctly separate worlds governed by wholly incommensurate rules. Ever since

Louis XIV decreed that the "Humanities" and "Sciences" be consigned to separate buildings,[2] the rift between poetic imagination and mathematical reasoning has not ceased to widen and has consolidated as something of a constitutive law of the human spirit. Evolving as parallels that sometimes repel, sometimes attract, but never intersect, the *two cultures*, as C.P. Snow called them, settled into mutually impervious and incomprehensible worlds. Gaston Bachelard, a poet who doubled as a mathematician, fancied he could describe these two sets of laws as the contents of radically separate spheres—each equally valid within its own scope and in its own terms— between which people could move as if from sleep to vigil, or vice-versa, switching one off in order to turn on the other.[3] The language of dreams does not contest that of equations, nor does the latter invade the terrain of poetry. So deep was the trench dug between these camps that some have sought to find anatomical grounds for it in the separation of the brain into two hemispheres, one creative and poetic, the other rational and ordering, and claimed to see in that bisectional structure a duality after the yin/yang divide of Chinese cosmology.[4] Moreover, they believed they had found in the predominance of one hemisphere over the other the root of all the woes of Western man. A somewhat mystical vision of Chinese characters championed in pedantic circles by Ezra Pound[5] lent the bi-hemispherical theory more than sufficient literary weight to make up for its lack of scientific ground. And then the "New Age" ideology came along and duly erected it as one of the pillars of wisdom.[6]

In this kind of light, good old Aristotle, alongside the

nefarious Descartes, emerged as the prototype of the rationalist headmaster who, ruler or leather strap in-hand, kept our inner Chinese strictly under wraps. Subscribers to such beliefs will react with astounded indignation to the idea I'm attributing to Aristotle here, for it presents a philosopher long cast as the guardian of schizophrenia as an apostle of unity. It contests a stereo-typical image which time and surface culture have sedi-mented as acquired truth. It reopens old wounds buried under the scar tissue of preconception.

This resistance is, of course, consummated fact, so all we can do is confront it, first by proving that the idea of unity of languages was Aristotle's all along, and second, that it is in fact an excellent idea, well worth being humbly revived by a civilization that put the ancient master's teachings out to pasture long before they had been properly examined. The best I can do here is give the reader general directions as to where proof of these two assertions should be sought.

Aristotle wrote *Poetics*, *Rhetoric*, a book on Dialectic (*The Topics*), and two treatises on Logic (*Prior Analytics* and *Posterior Analytics*), as well as two introductory works on language and thought in general (*Categories* and *On Inter-pretation*). These and Aristotle's other works all but vanished until the first century BCE, when one Andron-icus of Rhodes gathered them together in a new edition that forms the bedrock of our knowledge of Aristotle's philosophy today.

As with all posthumous editors, Andronicus had to impose some order upon the manuscripts, and the crite-rion he adopted in order to do that was to follow the division of the sciences, hence the *Corpus Aristotelicum* breaks down into *logics, theoretical sciences, practical sciences,* and *productive sciences.* This distinction has the merit of being made by Aristotle himself. But, as Octave Hamelin[7] so astutely observed, there is no reason to assume that the division of a philosopher's works into volumes should necessarily correspond, point-for-point, to his conception of the divisions within knowledge. Andronicus made just this assumption and grouped the manuscripts into these four categories. However, for want of other works that could fall under the "productive science" heading, he shoehorned in the *Poetics* and *Rhetoric,* thus cutting them off from the other treatises on the theory of discourse, now known as the six-volume *Organon,* Aristotle's set of logics, or introductions.

Among other things, this editorial decision yielded a prodigious number of consequences, and continues to do so to this day. First, right from Andronicus' maiden edition, the *Rhetoric*—a science detested by the philosophers as the emblem of their main adversaries, the Sophists—aroused zero philosophical interest. It was only read in schools of rhetoric, but even these, with the demise of democracy and enforced obsolescence of the orator, were in drastic decline. If rhetoric barely survived at all, it was only under the bell jar of narcissistic formalism.[8] Soon after that, the *Poetics* vanished from circulation only to reappear in the 16th Century.[9] These two occurrences may seem incidental and unimportant, until you bear in mind the following: the western Aristotelianism that developed over that vast period from the eve of the Christian Era all the way to the Renaissance, growing slowly at first, but accelerating from the 11th Century onwards, did so in complete ignorance of the *Rhetoric* and the *Poetics*. As our image of Aristotle is very much inherited from that period (seeing as the rediscovery of the *Poetics* during the Renaissance stirred some interest among poets and philologists, but none whatsoever in philosophical circles), what we speak of when we speak of Aristotle, whether in praise or blame, tends not to be the flesh and blood man, but a simplified schema assembled during the centuries when two of his major works still languished in oblivion. In particular, our idea of Aristotelian theory of discursive thought is exclusively based on the *Analytics* and the *Topics*, that is, on logic and dialectics, yet amputated from the foundations Aristotle had laid for them in the *Poetics* and the *Rhetoric*.[10]

But the mutilation did not end there. All that was left of the edifice of Aristotle's Theory of Discourse were the two top floors—the dialectic and logic—floating in the air like the poet's room in the Manoel Bandeira poem "Última canção do beco".[11] And it didn't take long for the third floor—the dialectic—to be ripped out too. As it merely dealt with probable demonstration, the dialectic was considered a lesser science, and was discarded in favor of analytical logic, cherished since the Middle Ages as the true key to Aristotle's thought. The image of an Aristotle that rested on the tripod of formal logic + sensuous cognition + theology of the Unmoved Mover took hold as true and incontestable history.

Not even rampant progress in biographical and philological studies inaugurated by Werner Jaeger[12] could change that. All Jaeger could do was debunk the myth of an Aristotle who'd been born the finished article and replace it with a more human vision of a thinker who evolved over time as his ideas matured. But the final product of that development, at least in the terms addressed in this book, was not all that different from the system set in stone throughout the Middle Ages, according to which the dialectic was a Platonic relic absorbed into and surpassed by analytical logic.

But there are facts that contest that vision. The first, noted by Eric Weil, is that the inventor of analytical logic never actually applied it in his own works, preferring to argue dialectically instead.[13] Secondly, Aristotle himself insists that logic does not generate knowledge, but can only help us verify the knowledge we have acquired, confronting it with the principles that underpin it in order to make sure it does not contradict them. When we lack those principles, the only way we can obtain them is through dialectical investigation, which, by comparing contrasting hypotheses, leads to a sort of intuitive enlightenment that brings those principles into evidence. In Aristotle, dialectic is, therefore, according to Weil, a *logica inventionis*, or logic of discovery: the true scientific method, of which formal logic is but a complement and means of final verification.[14]

However, if Weil's opportune intervention dispelled the myth of a total hegemony of analytical logic in Aristotle's system, it also neglected the matter of rhetoric. Twentieth-century academia still very much subscribed to the opinion of Sir David Ross, who, in turn, followed the view of Andronicus that the *Rhetoric* fulfills a "purely practical purpose"; that it "is not a theoretical work [...], merely a manual for the speaker".[15] To the *Poetics*, on the other hand, Ross attributed genuine theoretical value, without noticing that, if Andronicus had erred by placing it in the "Productive sciences" category, he may have been mistaken about the *Rhetoric*, too. After all, from the very moment it was rediscovered, the *Poetics* was primarily seen as a "practical manual" and so of more interest to the literati than to philosophers.[16] On the other hand, the *Topics* could arguably have been viewed as a "technical" or at least "practical" manual—as, at the Academy, that was precisely how dialectics functioned: as a set of practical norms for debate. In short, Andronicus' classification, followed to spec, generates endless confusion that could all be dispelled in one go simply by accepting the hypothesis, no matter how disturbing it may seem, that, as sciences of discourse, the *Poetics* and *Rhetoric* should really belong in the *Organon*, along with Aristotle's treatises on logic, rather than be considered "theoretical", or "practical", or even "productive" sciences. That is the core of the interpretation I argue for here, but it implies a profound revision of the traditional and still prevailing ideas concerning the Aristotelian science of discourse. It's a revision that could entail major consequences for how we view language and culture in general. Reclassifying works by a major philosopher may seem an innocent enough endeavor among erudite minds, but it is akin to shifting the columns of a building. You may need to demolish a lot of building work around them.

My reasons for justifying this change are:

I. The four sciences of discourse deal with the four ways in which one can, through words, influence others' minds (and one's own). The four modalities of discourse are characterized by their respective *levels of credibility*:

POETIC

Poetic discourse speaks of the possible (*dunatos*[17]), acting first and foremost upon the imagination, which grasps the possibilities which it, itself, envisages (*eikonízo*) or presumes (*eikastikos*, "presumable"; *eikasia*, "image", "representation").

RHETORICAL

Rhetorical discourse speaks of the true-to-nature (*pithanos*) and endeavors to persuade, to instill *firm belief* (*pistis*), and that, rather than any imaginative flights, requires acquiescence on the part of the listener. The speaker influences the other's will through persuasion (*peitho*), a psychological action grounded in shared beliefs. Where poetry creates an *impression*, rhetoric produces a *decision* as to the best or most convenient course of action to take based on the agreed set of accepted beliefs.

DIALECTICAL

Dialectical discourse, for its part, does not limit itself to suggesting or imposing beliefs, but to submitting them to proofs through trial and error, subjecting them to all manner of objections in order to see how well they stand up. It's a see-saw approach to thinking, operating transversally, always looking for truths among errors, and errors among truths (hence the *dia* part, which means "through", but also suggests duplicity and division). Dialectic is also sometimes referred to by the adjective *peirastic*, from the Greek root *peira* ("trial", "attempt", "endeavor". It's also the root of *peirasmos*, "temptation", and the terms em*pir*icism, ex*per*ience, etc., as well as the words "*pir*ate" [*peirates*], the living symbol of the adventurer, roaming the seas wherever the winds might blow him). Dialectical discourse therefore operates through hit and miss, eliminating hypotheses until it settles on what is most likely to be true. And it does this not according to how well they fit established beliefs, but in line with the higher demands of reason and reliable information.

ANALYTICAL

Logical or analytical discourse, on the other hand, starts with a universal premise which none would dispute in order to demonstrate (*apodexis*, "indestructible proof") the absolute truth of a conclusion through syllogistic deduction.

There is clearly a progressive scale of credibility here: from the possible, we reach the true-to-nature, the verisimilar; and from that, we step up a notch to the probable; and from the probable, we finally manage to attain demonstrable truth. The words Aristotle used to characterize the aims of each modality of discourse reveal that scalar quality: the difference between the four discourses is less one of *nature* than *degree*.

Possibility, verisimilitude, reasonable probability and *apodeictic truth* are, therefore, the key concepts upon which the four respective sciences are built: Poetics studies the means by which poetic discourse opens the imagination to the realm of the possible; Rhetoric, the means by which rhetorical discourse persuades the listener to come around to a desired belief; Dialectics, those by which dialectical discourse stress-tests beliefs held in order to ascertain their probable truth; and, finally, Logic (or Analytics), which studies the means by which one can arrive at apodeictic demonstrations of truth (*apo* "off", "away" + *deiknynai* "to show"), or scientific certainty. Now, these four basic concepts form a sort of nesting doll: the verisimilar must, evidently, stand within the bounds of the possible, just as the probable cannot fail to be true to nature, and so on. The consequence of that is so obvious it is quite startling that so few have noticed it: the four sciences are inseparable; they make no sense on their own. What defines them and differentiates them is not their respective sets of unique formal characteristics, but the four possible human attitudes in the face of discourse, four human reasons to speak and to hear: people speak in order to open the imagination to the immensity of the possible, to take some practical course of action, to critically examine the grounds of the beliefs that guide those actions, or to explore the consequences and ramifications of judgements already accepted as absolutely true, so that these can form the building blocks of scientific knowledge. *Discourse may be logical or dialectical, poetic or rhetorical, not in and of itself, or its internal structure, but in virtue of what it aims to achieve,* the human end to which it is put. That alone is what makes the four distinguishable, but by no means isolatable: each of these modalities *only is what it is* within the context of a culture, as the expression of human objectives. The modern notion of declaring one language *"poetry per se"* and another *"logic per se"* would have struck Aristotle as patently absurd. Worse than that: an alienating reification.[18] Aristotle had not yet been contaminated by the schizophrenia that has become the normal state of culture.

2. Yet Aristotle goes still further: he signals the different psychological dispositions corresponding to the listener of each of the four types of discourse, and this quaternity of dispositions reveals the same scale even more clearly:

(a) Listeners to a poetic discourse need to relax their expectations with respect to verisimilitude, as "it is probable that a thing may happen contrary to probability".[19] As such, Aristotle anticipates the *suspension of disbelief* which Samuel Taylor Coleridge would later describe as constituting "poetic faith". Admitting laxer criteria in terms of realism, readers (or viewers) accept that the misadventures befalling the tragic hero could well have happened to just about anyone, themselves included—in other words, that they are permanent human possibilities.

(b) In Ancient rhetoric, the listener was referred to as the *judge*, because he was expected to reach a decision, cast a vote or pass a sentence on the strength of what was heard. Aristotle, and the whole rhetorical tradition that came after him, accepted three different types of rhetorical discourse: *judicial* discourse, *deliberative* discourse and *epideictic* discourse (i.e., praise or blame for some figure or work, etc.)[20] In all three cases, the listener is called upon to decide something, whether the guilt or innocence of an accused; the benefit or detriment of a law or project; or the merits or demerits of an individual or thing. He is, therefore, consulted as an authority: the power of decision is his. If, in poetic discourse, the aim was to let the imagination take the reins of the mind and lead it on a flight of fancy from which no immediate practical result is to be expected, here it is the *will* that is called upon to listen to and judge the discourse so that a decision can be made that will lead to some concrete measure in the world of facts.[21]

(c) The interlocutor in dialectical discourse, on the other hand, is, on the inside, a participant in a dialectical process. Here, what is sought is not a decision, but the truth, or close enough to it, and the approximation can be slow, progressive, difficult, and tortuous, with no guarantee that a satisfactory result will be obtained. In this case, the listener should refrain from hasty decisions. In dialectic, the idea is not to persuade the other, as in rhetoric, but to reach a conclusion that both parties can agree is reasonable. Thus the interlocutors must contain any desire to win and be humbly prepared to change their own positions in the face of superior arguments. In dialectic, the participants do not defend positions, but explore hypotheses. Clearly this sort of dialogue is only possible if both parties know and accept the basic principles in accordance with which the issue is to be judged, and both must agree to engage honestly and respect the rules of dialectical demonstration. The key words here are impartiality, and, if necessary, self-critical resignation. Aristotle expressly warned his students against engaging in dialectical discussions with interlocutors not *au fait* or in agreement with the principles of the science: to do so would be to expose oneself to rhetorical broadsides that make a mockery of philosophy.[22]

(d) Finally, on the level of analytical logic, there is no more debate at all, only the linear demonstration of a conclusion that, based on premises accepted as evidently true, and proceeding rigorously by syllogistic deduction, cannot fail to be correct. Analytical discourse is a master's monologue. All the disciple can do is listen and admit the truth of it. Of course, if the demonstration fails, then the subject is resubmitted to the floor of dialectical discussion.[23]

From discourse to discourse, what we see is a progressive funneling, a narrowing-down of the admissible; from unlimited openness to the world of possibilities, we move to the more limited sphere of beliefs generally accepted by collective praxis. However, of that bundle of common-sense beliefs only a handful will stand the test of dialectical screening; only a smattering of those will be fed into analytical logic and come out the other end as irrefutably true, so that they can finally be adopted as the premises of scientifically valid reasoning. Each domain of discourse is therefore delimited by the one that came before it and the one that follows upon it. Imagined as concentric circles, they form the complete map of communications between civilized human beings, the sphere of possible rational knowledge.[24]

3. Lastly, Aristotle's theory of knowledge requires both scales. For Aristotle, knowledge begins with sensory data which are then transferred to memory and imagination (*phantasia, φαντασία*), where they are grouped into images (*eikoi*, or species, after the Latin *specieis*) according to their similarities. It is upon those images retained and organized by the faculty of *phantasia* that intelligence sets to work, not upon the sensory data itself. Intelligence sifts through these images and reorganizes them to create the eidetic schemas, or abstract concepts, about those species, on which judgements and ratiocinations will then be built. Between sensory experience and abstract reasoning, a dual bridge must be crossed: *phantasia* and so-called *simple apprehension*,[25] which captures isolated notions. There is no leap here; without the intermediation of *phantasia* and simple apprehension nothing can reach the upper stratum of scientific reasoning. There is perfect structural homology between this Aristotelian description of the cognitive process and the Theory of the Four Discourses. And it could not be otherwise: if the individual human being does not arrive at rational knowledge without first going through *phantasia* and simple apprehension, how could collective humanity—or the *polis*, or the more restricted circle of scholars—attain scientific certainty without prior and successive screening by poetic imagination, the organizing will that expresses itself in rhetoric and the dialectical filtering of philosophical discussion?

Once the *Rhetoric* and *Poetics* are summoned back from the "productive" or "poietic" exile to which they were sent by Andronicus and restored to their condition as philosophical sciences, the unity of the sciences of discourse leads us to a further, and surprising, verification: it contains a fully functioning Aristotelian philosophy of culture as the complete expression of the *logos*. In this philosophy, scientific reason emerges as the supreme fruit borne by the tree of poetic imagination, in turn rooted in the soil of sensible nature. And this sensible nature is not, for Aristotle, a mere irrational and hostile "exteriority", but the materialized expression of the divine *Logos*, i.e., culture, which, rising from myth-making earth to the zenith of scientific knowledge, comes to the fore as the humanized translation of this divine Reason, mirrored in miniature in the conscious mind of the philosopher. Aristotle effectively compares philosophical reflection with self-reflection of a God that consists, fundamentally, in self-awareness. The pinnacle of philosophical reflection, the crown of culture, is, in short, *gnosis gnoseos*, the knowledge of knowledge. Now, that plays out only at the instant when reflection encapsulates, in recapitulation, the entire process of its unfolding, that is, at the moment in which, having attained the sphere of scientific reason, it understands the unity of the four discourses through which it elevated progressively to this point. Only then is it ripe to transition from science or philosophy into wisdom and so into Metaphysics, which Aristotle, as Pierre Aubenque well discerned, prepared for, but never really brought to fruition, as its kingdom is not of this world.[26] The Theory of the Four Discourses is, *in this sense*, the beginning and end of Aristotelian philosophy. Beyond it, there is no more knowledge, in the strict sense, only the "science that is sought", the aspiration toward supreme wisdom, that *sophia* which, once attained, would mean both the realization and completion of philosophy.

2. An Aristotelian Model of Cultural History

THE VITALITY OF Aristotle's philosophy of culture can be measured through an obvious application and extension which Aristotle never actually gave to it himself, but which we can bestow in his name: the Theory of the Four Discourses does not merely describe a basic structure of the cultural world, but also its dynamic, or at least one of the fundamental principles of its evolution, which we might call *the principle of the succession of dominant discourses.*

This principle can be phrased as follows: *Each of the four discourses enjoyed a period of dominance throughout history, and the order in which those discourses succeeded to dominance accompanies a rising scale of credibility, from the poetic to the analytical.* By "dominance" I mean the implicit grounds for automatic credibility which the public invests in the ascendant class of discourse.

I. Poetic discourse emerged along with the first Oracles, back in the dark night of bygone time. It is the discourse *par excellence* of the sacerdotal caste and set the mold for The Vedas, the poetry of Homer, the Tao Te Ching and the Old Testament. It stands out for its "relatively little emphasis on a clear separation of subject and object: the emphasis falls rather on the feeling that the subject and object are linked by a common power or energy [...] this common energy of human personality and natural environment [...] Words in such a context are words of power or dynamic forces", and using them "may have repercussions in the natural order."[1]

2. Poetic discourse began to lose its authority in the West with the decline of the traditional Greek religion from the 7th Century BCE on, particularly with the advent of religious individualism and the cult of Dionysus, when poetry became an instrument for the expression of personal emotions, not necessarily shared with the wider community.[2] Rhetorical discourse began to rise to dominance at his time, especially with the establishment of the *polis* and, even more particularly, in the wake of Solon's reforms (6th Century BCE). Its practice was spread by the Sophists, the professional educators to the ruling class, whom they tutored in oratory. Rhetoric remained dominant throughout the Greek period and later in Rome, at least until the end of the Roman Republic (1st Century BCE), when it lost its *raison d'être*. As politics vanished from the public domain, oratory became something of a gratuitous endeavor. Once the structuring force of social consciousness, rhetoric was reduced to a mere subject of scholarly interest, and by the time of Quintilian (1st Century BCE) we were already well into the age of scholastic rhetoric, an ivory-tower occupation with no ties to active life.[3]

3. The advent of Christianity (a graft of Oriental origin) caused a glitch in this evolution, temporarily restoring poetic language to primacy. This second shine would last through to the end of the Patristic Period (5th Century CE). Soon, however, the Christian tradition would be sucked back into the general course of evolution.

4. Dialectical discourse, inaugurated by Socrates (5th Century BCE) and exemplified by Plato's dialogues, where it features as the supreme means of arbitration on all matters metaphysical, scientific, ethical, and political, did not become socially dominant (despite the spread of philosophical academies throughout the old world) until the end of the Patristic Period, after which it progressively became the basic instrument for unifying Christian doctrine with its defense against the heresies (surpassing the purely rhetorical arguments of the first exegetes, such as Tertullian). Dialectic reached the pinnacle of its prestige with the Great Scholastics of the 13th Century, when dialectical language was definitively assumed as the "official" garb of Christian thought. German idealism, some five centuries later, was a late dialectical rally in the face of the inexorable rise of the new science based on analytical logic.[4]

5. Logico-analytical discourse waited in the wings until the 16th Century, when classical rationalism a la Spinoza, Descartes, Malebranche and Leibniz began to impose the primacy of a wholly deductive science.[5] The new model would influence even Catholic theology: in the 18th

Century, the *Moral Theology* of Saint Alphonsus Liguori surged as a monument to deductivism on terrain one would normally think deeply hostile to such subject matter. Buoyed by advances in mathematics, deductivism would reach the height of its authority in the 20th Century, with the new theoretical physics of Einstein and Planck, mathematical logic, the success of information models, etc. The empire of science was the empire of analytical logic.[6]

6. With each shift in prestige, the outgoing discourse did not fall into disuse, but merely moved place, whereupon it would acquire new functions that would work deep-set changes upon its internal constitution:

(a) When rhetoric rose to prominence, poetic discourse ceased to be the language of a collective religion and became a mode of expression for individual sentiment. It also became aware of itself as just such a mode and so honed and perfected itself technically. Rather than the simple and natural grandeur of the epics, along came the delicate sophistications of Greek lyrical poetry.

(b) When the reign of rhetoric came to an end, it under went three core alterations:

- It became the subject of erudite systematization under Quintilian ("live" pursuits cannot be encapsulated within a closed schema, and, in comparison with the *corpus* of Quintilian, the *Rhetorics* of Aristotle and Cicero—directed toward a readership interested in their immediate practical application—begin to resemble mere provisory sketches).

- It was no longer widely used in political discourse or legal argumentation, but very much so in private communication (*ars dictandi*, the art of letter writing).

- It began to fuse with poetics, organizing a wide-ranging barrage of literary *topoi*, cliches, figures of thought and language for every occasion and aim, and from that mapping, as it were, modern literature[7] was born, and with it the whole Western concept of "literature" as an autonomous activity.

(c) With the rise of analytical discourse (especially after Napoleon founded the first Faculty of Science), dialectical discourse sought refuge in the field of History and the "humanities", hoping to preserve its privileges in opposition to the victorious advance of the logico-analytical method that would come to dominate the natural sciences. There was a dual result to this: on one hand, the formation of the "human sciences"; on the other, with Hegel and Marx, the elevation of dialectic to an all-encompassing philosophy of history. This gave rise to a similarly twofold conflict that remained current into the century just ended, at least up until the 1970s, with the dispute between the human and natural sciences, on one side, and between the Marxists and neo-positivists, on the other.[8]

The fate of poetic discourse in a world ruled by analytical logic is at once interesting and tragic. Initially, poetics became increasingly self-aware as a body of linguistic means, enabling "literature" to gradually acquire a certain autonomy as cultural expression. Later, with Mallarmé and Joyce, that autonomy was taken to its ultimate consequences: literary form proclaimed its independence from all "content", severing its ties with the world of human experience and knowledge. This "closing in on itself" of poetics, which was in part a radical and desperate protest against the primacy of analytical discourse, lends certain works of 20th-century literature an enigmatic tone that simulates mystery, the magic language of primitive oracular poetry. But it is individual expression, with no public authority, and nobody expects it to wield any power over nature. It is, therefore, an "empty" oracle, a purely conceptual oracular form with no actual oracular power.[9] It's the end of a cycle.

The Theory of the Four Discourses implicitly contains a comprehensive descriptive model of cultural history that can be fruitfully applied to other civilizations. For example, in the Islamic world, the initial oracular phase begins with the Quranic revelations and the words of the Prophet; soon afterwards come the parties, each with its own rhetoric;[10] the proliferation of rhetorical discourses, in turn, creates the need for dialectical triage, which comes with Al-Kindi, Al-Ghazzali, Avicenna; and, finally, Islamic theology organizes itself into a deductive system thanks to the great orthodox commentators, such as Bukhari. In the 20th century, the theology of the fundamentalist movement leads to abstract and extreme consequentialism, for example, with Sayyid Qutb and his thirty-volume *In the Shade of the Qu'ran*—the equivalent in structure (not content, naturally) of Saint Alphonsus' *Moral Theology.*

That this theory—a descriptive rather than explicative causal model—might have such profound elucidative power when applied to the historical evolution of civilizations should come as no surprise, seeing as Aristotle invented the concept of *organic evolution,* by which the identity of a substance is not gleaned from its static form but derives from the template in accordance with which its transformations occur over time—the dialectic of permanence through change. Aristotle was also the herald of genetic explanation, not only in the natural sciences but in the history of thought. It's an intrinsic demand of dialectical method; each of Aristotle's treatises begins with a historical sketch in which the present state of an issue is explained by virtue of how the debate upon it has evolved over time—and that makes Aristotle the inventor of the "History of Science" as a genre. Therefore there's really nothing odd at all about the fact that he should give rise to a new model for the history of culture after all these centuries.

What is strange is that the Aristotelian vision of the unicity of culture has been overlooked for so long, without any of those pining for lost unity having thought to look for it in Aristotle, preferring instead to seek it in China.[11]

3. The Presence of Aristotelian Discourse in Western History

I T HAS ALREADY BEEN SAID in earlier lectures[1] that this
course is based on an original idea of Aristotle's that
remained embedded and effectively hidden in his corpus
through the centuries, and which had to be unearthed
and brought back into the light of day, so that we might
derive from it the principles of a new educational
method.[2]

We all know that Aristotle wrote a Poetic, a Rhetoric, a
treatise on Dialectics (*Topics*) and a suite of works on
Logic, or Analytical Demonstration, as he preferred to call
it, subsumed under the general title of *The Organon*.

We also know the importance Aristotle's ideas have
held in the development of Western thought, and are
aware that these books have, for the last two thousand
years, served as the model and framework for an infinity
of ideas and creations of the European mind. Naturally,
such pivotal works must also have extended their scope of
influence to education, and it can be safely said that

generations upon generations of philosophers and scientists have been schooled on *The Organon*, while similar legions of poets, orators, playwrights and novelists have absorbed countless cardinal rules of their crafts from the *Poetics* and *Rhetoric*. Aristotle is, without doubt, one of the fathers of European culture, alongside his teacher and colleague, Plato. In order to truly gauge the magnitude of the influence these two Greeks have had in the formation of our culture, all we need do is bear in mind that the other pair of crucial formative forces behind it were collective endeavors, sedimented over centuries of experience, namely Roman Law and Judeo-Christian Theology. In the origin of European culture, the contribution these two philosophers made stands shoulder to shoulder with the importance and durability of the legacies left by two whole civilizations.

However, despite its momentousness, down through the centuries Aristotle's influence has followed a developmental line that, when examined up-close, strikes me as odd and abnormal. We shall soon see why that is. But even stranger than the abnormality itself is the fact that historians have generally failed to notice it.

In order to sketch this bizarre phenomenon in broad strokes, I must first take a step backwards and speak a little of Aristotle's gnoseology, or philosophy of knowledge and cognition.

It is widely known that, in the centuries-old debate between the empiricist and rationalist gnoseologies, Aristotle's own occupies an intermediary position which, for want of a better term, is called *intellectualist*. This midpoint has been frequently misinterpreted, such that Aristotle has often been categorized—depending on the occasion— as being anything from a full rationalist to the father of the empiricists.

The prototype of the pure rationalist was Spinoza, according to whom solitary reasoning, operating entirely according to its own laws and independently of any external data, could attain to the highest truths, while experience could yield but uncertain, accidental knowledge.

In diametric opposition to Spinoza is John Locke, the apostle of radical empiricism. For Locke, man is born a *tabula rasa*, a blank page, on which successive experiences imprint their images, until, through mere accumulation of similar experiences, these images begin to arrange themselves into patterns, or concepts, in a system we call "reason". In other words, reason derives from experience.

Aristotle's so-called intellectualism consists in attributing interconnected and complementary functions to reason and experience, such that neither can claim primacy when it comes to the origin of knowledge.

Be that as it may, there's no static equilibrium between reason and experience, because Aristotle invented a concept that would go on to be one of the most fruitful in the history of philosophy and the sciences, namely *organic development*, according to which one can only really know a thing or phenomenon thoroughly if one studies its genesis and the progressive development of its internal structures. So, when Aristotle broaches the problem of knowledge, for example, he describes the origin and development of the human cognitive apparatus in such a manner as both the empiricist and rationalist perspectives fit harmoniously within it as phases and aspects of the cognitive process. It was only when we lost from view this unity of knowledge as the potential of a living form that grows and develops that the whole empiricist-versus-rationalist debate arose and Aristotle, oblivious to the whole debacle, started being enlisted into the opposing camps.

To couch it in Aristotelian terms: we can only understand, and perhaps resolve, a dispute when we investigate the common ground from which the antagonist parties emerged; this exploration of the origins generally ends up revealing the adversaries to be nothing more than "quarreling siblings". In fact, in Aristotle we see an initial synthesis whose elements would separate centuries later, polarized in the antagonism between empiricists and rationalists.

According to Aristotle, all human knowledge derives, temporally, from *sensations*. If the five senses didn't ply us with data from the world around us we would have nothing at all to know. Yet all animals have sensations, and in this aspect know as much as we do. Therefore, if some animals know more than others, the difference can't lie in the senses, but in some other function possessed in greater or lesser levels of development. For Aristotle, this function is *memory*.[3] Humankind has the richest, most exceptional memory in the animal kingdom, which is why we know more than the other animals.

So far, so empiricist. However, for Aristotle, memory is not just a passive recording faculty. It is imaginative too, capable of blending images to create new patterns. Memory and imagination are, for Aristotle, one and the same faculty, which he calls *phantasia,* and it switches function depending on whether the same images are being repeated, or different images are being combined to form an inexhaustible plethora of concoctions. A simple image retained in memory, reproducing a thing or fact, Aristotle calls a *phantasma* (no macabre connotations implied). As *phantasmata* accumulate, *phantasia* begins to behave creatively, recombining them, schematizing them, sifting them and simplifying them until all those similar to one another have been condensed into a single image. Imagination organizes the contents of memory by aligning the myriad *phantasmata* into synthetic images, or schemas, which designate things kind for kind, rather than unit for unit. As such, in order to recognize a thing as a "cow", we don't need to be able to recall every single cow we've seen, one by one, which would make the work of intelligence inviable, but simply conjure in the imagination a schematic image of "cow" that stands in for "all" cows, or, put in more technical terms, the *species* of cow. This prototype is what Aristotle calls the "essence" of the species "cow", and it synthetically encompasses all cows, everywhere. Hardly coincidentally, the Greek word Aristotle uses here, *eidos,* means both "essence" and "image", while the Latin term *species* also means "class of similar things" *and* "sight, view, appearance" (hence words like "spectacles", for example). Imagination is therefore the bridge between sensory knowledge and logical thought.

Essentially, logical thought consists of coherency among schemas. It is a vast structuring of relationships of contiguity, succession, pertinence, opposition, similarity, difference, hierarchical layering, etc. How could it execute all these operations upon the inexhaustible variety of sensory data *directly*? If these data were not previously selected, summarized and simplified in memory and imagination, we would need divine powers of mind to herd that boundless multiplicity of information streaming through our senses into anything resembling a logical framework. But logical thought does not operate upon perception directly at all, merely upon the pre-selected and simplified essence stored in memory as schema or *species*.

This is how we arrive at that supreme achievement of logical thought: the *concept*. In a single mental operation, the concept encompasses not just the species of things, but the species of relationships between things, and, on a higher level, the species of species, i.e., genera, to which these belong. And so, genus after genus, concepts can scale further up to more general and universal relations and even to merely possible relations and grades of possibility that determine the hierarchy across which possibilities exist.

Yet the concept is nothing more than a purely verbal (albeit unexpressed) schema that simplifies still further the sensory schema under which memory has already subsumed a certain species of beings. In other words, thinking only acts from a certain level of generality up. Hence the strategic importance of imagination; for the five senses, all that exists is the here and now, the concrete case, the immediately given; for thinking, all that exists is the concept, the general, the schema of schemas, each more rarefied and universal than the last. Without imaginative mediation, these two cognitive faculties would be separated by a yawning gulf. Humankind would perhaps have sensations just like a common rabbit, and might manage to think something, much like a computer, but we would be incapable of thinking about what we felt; that is, we would be unable to reason about lived experience, or, on the other side of the equation, steer experience with reasoning in pursuit of new knowledge. The human mind would be as efficient as a computer operated by a rabbit, and as alive as a rabbit pixel-drawn on a computer screen.

Logical thinking would not be possible without the help of this maligned, disdained faculty, so often dismissed as the playpen of children and the padded cell of the insane: imagination. When, through imaginative mediation, what was *presented* to us by the senses becomes *representation*—the image repeated by me to myself—then, and only then, does it become possible to *think*. Often, while meditating on this, I have verified that it is indeed a miracle, or, if you prefer, a paradox. While, for thought, only the generic exists, and the generic is nothing in particular; for the senses, the image is always of something singular and concrete. But imagination produces a strange hybrid, a species that is at once singular and generic. To the senses, a cow is a cow. In thought, the concept of a cow is not a cow, only a mental schema of cowness. In the imagination, however, "a cow" is, at once, one cow, or many cows, or a cow that is *all* cows; and it is from this bizarre overlap that the connection between logical thought and lived reality derives. It was a role that, much later, Richard and Hugh of Saint Victor would recognize in what they called *imaginatio mediatrix* — "mediating imagination". And, many centuries after that, Benedetto Croce would confess: "If man were not a fantastical animal, he would not be a logical one either".[4] In Greek and medieval cosmologies, imagination, or fantasy, was always understood as being to the human microcosm what the World Soul was on the cosmic scale; it is through the World Soul that the eternal archetypes contained in the Divine mind or in *Logos* descend to earth and become real living things. And, in the Christian world, the World Soul was identified with the Holy Virgin, the Mother of the *Logos* incarnate. Aristotelian theory of imagination lies at the root of all of that.

So, according to Aristotle, experience amounts to a progressive series of sifting, selection, and structuring that begins in the senses (in experience) and culminates in the rational organization of knowledge, which, in turn, rationally organizes action to foster new forms of experience, and round and round it goes. As each faculty on the cognitive scale comes into play, it conducts its own selection, sifting the essential from the accidental and inserting the derived knowledge into an increasingly ample, more cohesive and functional framework. Knowledge does not come from experience, nor is it imposed by reason. It derives from the rational structuring of experience deposited in memory and decanted by the imagination; a structuring that settles on the one hand into the constitution of humankind as a biological creature, and, on the other, into the universal ontological principles intuitively grasped, and reflected in diverse ways, in the forms of the four discourses. For Aristotle, knowledge is a unitary, organic process that progressively elevates from the elementary forms shared by humans and animals to the ultra-complex syntheses of science and philosophy.

This unity, this organic character of knowledge, is the backbone of Aristotle's gnoseology. It is a legacy that, whilst abandoned during the centuries-long dispute between rationalists and empiricists, was taken up anew in the 20th Century by Maurice Pradines in his "law of reciprocal genesis" of the cognitive faculties;[5] by Jean Piaget,[6] in his genetic theory of the logical structures; and, to a more limited extent, Noam Chomsky, in his generative grammar. The Aristotelian seed continues to bear fruit.

But the unity of the cognitive process in Aristotle is the result or expression of the unity of man himself. Aristotle's gnoseology stems from his anthropology, his conception of humankind.

Humans are, for Aristotle, rational animals. Rational animality is the very definition or essence of humankind. Animality and rationality are fused in the human being in an essential and inseparable way. Our description of the cognitive process as Aristotle saw it is nothing more than the narrative of the ascent of purely animal—that is, sensory—knowledge to rational and thus properly human knowledge. But we're not dealing here with what Engels called a *transition of the animal into man*, but a perfect, seamless continuity operated through a mutation that does nothing but reveal, in the final form acquired by a being through its own development, the essence that was there from the very outset, steering it unseen.[7]

This needs to be understood in the light of Aristotle's theory of potency (form) and act (matter). "Act" means actual, patent, materialized; while "potency" is the potentiality behind the act. Potency is dependent upon actuality, not the other way round. All power is the power to manifest agency in acts of power, which is why potency cannot be considered independently of act. Act, on the other hand, is act regardless of potency (hence Aristotle's definition of the supreme power, God, as "Pure Actuality").

So while Aristotle defines man as a rational animal, he does not mean to say that all humans are rational all of the time, nor that reason is an "impotent potential" incapable of coming to fruition. On the contrary: humanity *as a species* is defined by the potency of reason and the degree to which the individual endeavors to bring that potential into act, and has *the capacity* to do so. Humans may find themselves, by whatever accidental cause, deprived of the means required to realize this reason *in potentia*, but the human *species* is human precisely because this potential tends (in both senses of the term) to realize itself in act. (For Aristotle, *privation* is an abnormality, and species are expressed by what is most normal or normative to them.)

We might say that a newborn baby "isn't yet" rational, but that rationality lies dormant or latent within. That said, potential reason is still reason, and nothing else, because it is a potential that tends to convert into act. As such, the history of the genesis of human knowledge is none but that of the history of the *passage of human reason from potency into act*. The journey from sensory data to *phantasia*, and from that to rational knowledge occurs without rupture, a smooth progressive realization of the rational potency already embedded in our sensations. In a homologous and complementary manner, the sensorial form of each material thing comes imbued with the expression of the inner principle of its organization, which is what constitutes its intelligibility. Through a succession of abstractive refinements, knowledge grasps the intelligible *in* the sensible (not beyond it or above it, as in Platonism).

However, as, in Aristotelian metaphysics, each being has an *entelechy*,[8] or immanent finality, that defines it from within and directs it towards its fullest realization, naturally reason, as an *entelechy*, guides human change from the outset of cognitive development all the way to the most complete manifestation of our defining potential. In other words, reason does not "arise" suddenly, out of nowhere, overriding the imagination and sensations, but has been there all along, latent, imbricated and active in sensibility and, later, in *phantasia*. Karl Marx, a major admirer of Aristotle, drew out the conclusion implicit to this gnoseology when he observed that, in humankind, sensory knowledge is more than just a simple animal function, but is—and is from the outset—*human* sensitivity.[9] Maurice Pradines went still further, with a grandiose attempt to describe the hidden steerings of latent rational intelligence within sensibility, like some secret, inbuilt compass guiding the newborn's first tentative actions.[10] People are not only rational when they reason, but also, implicitly, when they sense and imagine. They could never humanize if they were not already human from the start.

This brief description of Aristotle's gnoseology and anthropology would benefit from an elucidation of his cosmology, which pictures a cosmos stacked in hierarchical levels descending from Divine Reason to the creatures of the sensory world. This reveals the genesis of human knowledge as a sort of inverted and dialectically complementary image of the world's structure. However, to do his cosmology any justice would require far more space than I presently have at my disposal, and knowledge of it is not essential to a clear understanding of what I aim to present here.

Namely, the inevitable conclusion that, if Aristotle's cognitive process is an organic unity that starts in sensations, filters through imagination, ascends into thought and culminates in the rational organization of the world, without either leaps or discontinuities, then the method of knowledge, *The Organon* or methodological instrument that structures scientific activity, must also have a cohesive unicity, the expression of an organism in unbroken evolution. It should encompass all the modalities of knowledge, from the sensory to the rational, and operate all the connections, transitions, conversions and devolutions that take place between them, and do so in such a manner as we can see the stages unfurling one from the other without rupture. Toward this end, *The Organon* should contain, prior even to a logic *per se*, a "logic of imagination", without which the framework of the sciences would risk descending into a mere bundle of formal schemas with no connection whatsoever to the reality of experience. Otherwise put, and thinking more in terms of the pedagogical aspect of *The Organon*: shouldn't the wise man's education begin with the discipline of imagination?

However, when we examine Aristotle's methodological writings, *The Organon* as we know it today, namely in Andronicus of Rhodes' canonical form, repeated in all the later editions of the *Corpus Aristotelicum*, we see that it begins with rational knowledge and works upwards, into the science of concepts, as if these were *causa sui,* in no way predicated upon a science of images. Compared with Aristotle's gnoseology, anthropology, and cosmology, his methodology seems like a sculpted bust floating in the air, with neither body nor pedestal.

We must not forget that many of Aristotle's works have been lost. The history of Aristotle's manuscripts reads like an adventure novel in which most of the characters end up dead or disappeared. Perhaps a methodology of imaginative knowledge ranks amongst the latter. Whatever the truth of it may be, all that has come down to us today as an Aristotelian methodology is *The Organon*. That, and nothing else.

Even so, and such as it is, *The Organon* has exercised enormous influence on philosophy, the sciences and education down through the centuries, without anyone ever thinking to ask what happened to imaginative knowledge, so pivotal to the overall schema of Aristotle's philosophy. Throughout the Middle Ages, *The Organon* served the function it was intended to fulfill in the higher teaching of philosophy—that of both tool and primer—so the fact that it opened onto the sciences and philosophy, but not imaginative knowledge, caused no surprise. After all, why would it have, at a time when the arts were just as developed as philosophy and in which the principles of architecture (to mention just one of the arts) bore such a close relation to the principles of logical thought?[11]

At the same time, since Antiquity at least, people had continued to read the *Rhetoric* and *Poetics* (the latter to a lesser extent, as we shall see), but as though neither had anything at all to do with *The Organon*, and were simply side projects of a more practical than theoretical persuasion which the great Greek sage had decided to pursue in his spare time, as a sort of respite from his "serious" philosophical labors.

Without doubt, the *Rhetoric* and *Poetics* drew a different sort of readership, while the hardened philosophers pored over *The Organon,* and the treatises on Physics and Metaphysics, such "literary" matters were left to the more imaginative, less intellectual sorts, who would be out of their depth with the logics.

The *Rhetoric* continued to attract interest, but less among philosophers than grammar teachers. Even the work's political importance diminished over time. As the old democracy disappeared, giving way to more centralizing regimes, orators were now surplus to requirements, as public debate became a thing of the past. Cut off from its lifeworld, the *Rhetoric* became a merely didactic exercise.

The *Poetics* fared even worse and was all but forgotten by the end of Antiquity, only to be rediscovered in the late Middle Ages. According to the eminent philologist Segismundo Spina, "The *Poetics* can't have been well-known in Antiquity. Even Horace, whose *Ars Poetica* is clearly inspired by the Greek philosopher's treatise, does not appear to have known Aristotle's *Poetics* directly".[12] Some interest in it still lingered in the East: a Syriac version appeared in the 6th Century, and it was translated into

Arabic in the 11th. In the West, only during the Renaissance did "Aristotle's *Poetics* become a subject of curiosity, with editions, studies and translations being made... The classical aesthetic developed throughout the 16th Century in Italy was largely based on Aristotle's little code".[13] The first work to recall the treatise appears to have been a commentary on it by Francesco Robortelli, published in 1548.

A growing number of translations and commentaries ensued, and the influence of the *Poetics* rose accordingly, to the point that it became the foundation upon which the debates for and against the classical aesthetic took place between the 16th and 18th Centuries. Curiously, this interest was restricted mainly to poets, playwrights and literary theorists, and failed to spark a similar response among hard-nosed philosophers, who were not only underwhelmed about the resurgence of the *Poetics* but began to turn away from the Aristotle they'd long known, spurred in large measure by the rebellion against the Scholastics gathering momentum in the wake of the burgeoning modern philosophy of Descartes, Bacon, Newton, Galileo, and Leibniz. This philosophy, which was driven by a new concept of experience (the mathematizable experience of Galileo as opposed to the old criterion of immediate sense data defended by the Scholastics), was taking increasingly divergent paths to medieval thought (and, therefore, to Aristotle, at least as the Middle Ages had understood him). There is no shortage of historians who have interpreted the development of Renaissance philosophy and science as a liberation from the Aristotelian yoke after fifteen centuries of servitude.

What an odd way of looking at it! The Renaissance, as the whole world knows, derived from a revaluing of literature, poetry and rhetoric, which came to enjoy a level of cultural import they'd been denied during the Middle Ages, when academic philosophy had reigned supreme. This re-appreciation came with, and partly because of, the rediscovery of Aristotle's *Poetics*, allowing the Greek to re-emerge as the patron of the literary renaissance at the same time as he was dethroned as the lord of science.

But the strangest part of all this is the following. Whilst the Middle Ages found nothing concerning imaginative knowledge in Aristotle, it cultivated this modality of knowledge and elevated it to perfection, as we can see from the whole aesthetic of the Victorines,[14] Saint Thomas Aquinas,[15] Saint Bonaventure, and in the pedagogical synthesis of the Liberal Arts that would give Dante Alighieri the formula for artistic perfection: the truths of the Quadrivium conveyed through the Trivium.[16] In short, the Medieval world is utterly incomprehensible without reference to a type of imaginative, symbolic thought, which, nevertheless, would seem to have developed in the absence of Aristotle's aesthetic ideas, which would only be rediscovered in the 1700s. The advent of modern science overlaps neatly with the dissolution of this symbolic thinking, which, at the threshold of modernity, was swiftly replaced by a classificatory system with a purely logical-analytical base.[17]

Perhaps that is why Aristotle's *Poetics* was understood in a strikingly rationalist sense, to the point that the classic poetics of the 16th and 17th Centuries went down in history as synonymous with formalist rigor and ferocious control over the imaginary. But can we really interpret Aristotle in this sense, or is this merely Aristotle as seen by a rationalist century?

Whatever the answer might be, the succession of episodes recounted here marks one of the most intricate stages in the development of Western thought, yet it is far from ever having been elucidated by the historians. In fact, most of them never even noticed anything strange about one Aristotle entering into decline just as another rose; about the arts ascending (over pure philosophy) at the same time as symbolic language disappeared or lost all value; about a rationalist aesthetic being erected precisely upon an author who valued imaginative knowledge as the precondition for rational knowledge—all of this creates such a densely tangled knot that we can straightaway chuck out the whole "Middle Ages versus Renaissance" schema, identified as "Aristotelianism versus modern science". The transformations that occurred during that time were by no means uniform. Rather, they were, in many cases, from the arts to science, philosophy to religion, varied, confused, and even contradictory. Above all, the history of Aristotle's influence loses its apparent linearity, and becomes embroiled in a skein of contradictions.

However, if we look to the other side of the world, to the East, from where Aristotle's works returned to us in Arabic from the 11th Century on, we will see that things took a rather different course there. There were confusions too, naturally enough, such as mistaking a Neo-Platonic Theology as a work of Aristotle's for a few centuries, but the point of interest to us is that, in Islamic philosophy, Aristotle was understood in a very different way, and we ought perhaps to look to its readings of Aristotle in search of a solution to some of the conundrums outlined above. That, however, is really a task for the historians. For our purposes, suffice it to underscore the following: in Islamic philosophy, at least *a general idea of Aristotle's integral methodology was retained*, uniting imaginative and rational knowledge. The loss of this to the West —which still needs to be explained—may well lie at the root of the confusions I drew out above.

Avicenna, for example, explicitly states that Aristotelian logic—*The Organon*—includes a *Poetics*, *Rhetoric*, *Dialectic*, Logic *per se*, and Sophistical Refutations.

Avicenna couldn't be clearer: he places the *Poetics* and the *Rhetoric* squarely within *The Organon*, along with the *Topics* and *Analytics*, etc. Avicenna says little else on the subject, but what he did say is already enough to show that he understood the unity of the science of discourse in Aristotle along much the same lines that interest us here.

The West, alas, did not. Western philosophers focused their attentions on the *Logic* and the *Dialectic*, leaving the *Rhetoric* and *Poetics* to the grammar teachers...With that, all vision of the organic unity of Aristotle's method was lost.[18] The amputated part relegated to the background avenged itself later on, returning to prominence in the garb of classical aesthetics during the Renaissance, while, in the field of philosophy, the new science steadily buried the Scholastic version of Aristotelian logic and dialectics. Ironies of history.

4. The Universal Typology of the Discourses

ONCE AGREED THAT, for Aristotle,[1] there are four fundamental types of discourse, all that remains to ask is whether he is right in that assertion; whether there might not be three, or five, or ninety, and if, rather than their reciprocal arrangement, a different order based on another set of relations might not be more beneficial. In short, it remains to ascertain which arguments we might draw upon in defense of the Aristotelian conception that were not proposed—and perhaps not even fore-glimpsed—by Aristotle himself. We must demonstrate the *logical necessity* of the hypothesis of the four discourses, preferably by approaching the theme from a different angle to the Stagirite, so that we might obtain the same result by different means. And if there is an approach which Aristotle invented, but hardly ever used, it is the analytical-demonstrative method. So, *a la* Spinoza, I will reason by pure deduction, *more geometrico*, and show that this route leads to the same results that philology suggests through textual interpretation and dialectic sustains through the exclusion of contrary hypotheses.

I. Fundamental Concepts

1. All discourse is movement, the *passing* from one proposition to another. There is a beginning and an end, premises and a conclusion, with a developmental progression along the way. The formal unity of any discourse depends on its propositional unity, that is, the arrangement of the various parts with a view towards obtaining the desired conclusions.

2. The *premise* is that which is taken as given or agreed, and which, as such, is not in discussion itself. There are explicit and implicit premises: the former are mentioned at the beginning of, or within, the discourse, while the latter are not openly declared. The omission of premises can be intentional or not. Proponents may have beliefs so deeply entrenched and ingrained that they inadvertently take them as premises. These are called *presuppositions*, and they are not the same as intentionally omitted premises.

3. Propositional unity manifests through the fact that the component parts of an argument should be connected logically, analogically, chronologically, etc. I call this connection *formal unity*, with the reservation that various kinds of connection in the same argument can serve the same propositional unity.

4. The purpose of every discourse is to provoke a modification in the listener, however tenuous or fleeting that might be. By modification, I mean change of opinion;

receipt of information; or arousal of an emotion. We are modified by all of these in their own ways.

5. The listener's acceptance of the proposed modification testifies to the argument's *credibility*.

6. The listener's willingness to consider the argument in the first place is what I call *initial credibility*, as it requires at least provisional acceptance of the premises. *Final credibility* is the full acceptance of the proposed modification. Initial credibility requires provisional acceptance of the premises and is itself a premise. Final credibility consists in full admission of the conclusions and, implicitly at least, the ramifications deriving therefrom.

7. *Definition of discourse* — with the premise already believed, we can consider the conclusions believable. Discourse is, therefore, *the passage from the believed to a believable ramification through a chain of connections*.

8. An effective argument is one which achieves final credibility, while a failed argument is one that fails in converting initial credibility into final credibility and so ends in the rejection of the proposed modification (which is a modification in its own right, only negative, or contrary).

9. Every argument or discourse aims for positive final credibility.

10. These concepts, principles and criteria apply to all discourses, across all possible genres: from parliamentary oratory to lyric poetry, news broadcasts to philosophical treatises, a parent's telling-off of a child to a company's annual report to its shareholders. The theory outlined in the following sections will demonstrate this universal applicability.

II. Possibility of a universal typology of discourses

Typology is a differentiation according to extremes or poles. Every typology is couched in maximum differences, which could be purely ideal and therefore impossible to encounter in practice. In these cases, the real elements will only ever be approximations to the posited extremes.

Can there be a typology of discourses aprioristically deduced from the very concept of discourse itself? The infinity of existing discourses—to say nothing of possible discourses—as well as their unassailable variety of forms, motives, subjects and styles, would suggest the answer is no. However, the concept of discourse—the transition from believed a to believable b—already includes the idea of a maximum and a minimum: because the believed premise is, at the outset, the maximally believed, while the believable is, at the conclusion, upgraded to a new believed content. So, without a scale that runs from the maximally believed (the limit of the credible accepted thus far) to the minimally believable (the simple theoretical possibility of something becoming a new belief), there can be no argument at all. The scale of credibility— either of premises or of conclusions—is a *condition of the possibility of the existence of discourse*. This scalar character of credibility shows that a theoretical and *a priori* typology of discourses is not only possible, but necessary. If discourses were not scaled per credibility, there could be no discourses at all.

This raises a question: should the scale be based on the credibility of the premises or of the conclusions? Obviously, the answer is on the credibility of the premises, because the credibility of the conclusions depends on them. As the conclusion of one argument can become the premise of another argument as soon as it is accepted, it follows that there is a *scale of premises* and that the steps in that scale give rise to the steps in the scale or theoretical typology of discourses.

III. Scale of premises

Regardless of the subject matter, the totality of possible premises encompasses a scale that runs from maximally believable to minimally believable.

MAXIMUM
(certain, true)

MINIMUM
(possible)

The maximum degree of credibility is that attributed to the irrefutably true or certain. I'm speaking here from a formal and functional perspective; it really doesn't matter if the maximally believed premise *really is true* or certain in its content (materially true, that is), only that it be *taken as true* in the argument. On the scale of *veracity*, the opposite of the absolutely true is the absolutely false. However, on the scale of *credibility*, which is what interests us here, if the maximum degree of credibility pertains to the absolutely true—or what is taken to be so—the minimum degree cannot be attributed to the absolutely false, because that which is recognized as false cannot be taken as a premise for anything at all, precisely because it is refuted out of hand. To say that something is false is to reject it as a premise, and therefore also dismiss any argument that might be derived from or based upon it; and that, apart from cases of logical demonstration *ad absurdum*, means it has no relevance whatsoever to the typology of discourses. In demonstrations *ad absurdum*, for their part, the recognizably false is permissible hypothetically as a premise only in order to reveal the absurdity of any conclusions that might originate from it. So, even in this case, the credibility of the premise (in this case, zero) is what underpins the possibility of the discourse. As such, the minimally credible—the lowest notch on our scale—is not the same as the false, because the false is not even minimally credible. Whatever is unbelievable therefore lies outside our scale of credibility. If the maximum degree corresponds to the absolutely true, the minimum degree corresponds to the *minimally true*, that is, to the *merely possible*. Anything less than that is, by definition, impossible, and therefore not worthy of the slightest belief, because it is demonstrably false, and does not register on our scale.

The typology of possible discourses therefore begins with the polarization of premises (and therefore of the discourses based thereon) on a spectrum that runs between the *maximally credible* (or absolutely *true*) and *minimally credible* (or merely *possible*).

The typology would end there, were it reducible to a

simple linear scale; the other types of discourse would have to be positioned arbitrarily along that spectrum in accordance with some attributed degree of credibility, or —we might imagine—on the strength of some empirical examination of the variety of *de facto* discourses that exist, which would be an endless labor resulting in innumerable intermediary types. So, either the scale ends there, or we need to find another pair of extremes, a second polarity that, in conjunction with the first (maximum and minimum credibility), produces a system of maximally irreducible cardinal directions: this system of four directions transforms the *scale* (simple quantitative grading) into a *typology* (qualitative differentiation).

IV. The four discourses

If every discourse is movement, departing from one thing in order to arrive at another, and if we exclude the possibility of any infinite discourse, which would embark from the absolute beginning of all things, travel through all possible things, and arrive at the absolute end of all things, we can also conclude that *every argument is a segment*. As such, arguments can be prolonged indefinitely, either backwards—towards the final grounds of its premises— or forwards, in an indefinite series of ramifications.[2] What limits any given discourse to a certain span— bookending backwards by taking the premises not yet discussed as presuppositions, and forwards, by renouncing consequences that extend beyond a certain point—is simple human decision. Of course, we might accept universal principles that would lend sustenance to arguments at their farthest anterior extreme, but that changes nothing, because, by working backwards to a universal principle an argument does not encounter any limit beyond which it would be *impossible* to continue working further backwards, it merely runs up against the limits of evidence and obviousness, beyond which going any further would be *unnecessary* (though not impossible). Any argument that bores back towards some first foundation could continue indefinitely, even if, in doing so, it rendered itself *redundant*, indefinitely exploring the already known and repeating the already evident. On the other hand, the indefinite progression of consequences could perhaps breach the limits of the humanly thinkable, or at least verifiable, but, theoretically, that alone would not oblige it to stop anywhere at all along the line. So, there is an unlimited extension at the beginning, trailing off into an ocean of evidence of first principles, and, at the other extreme, an indefinite extension of unverifiable or irrelevant consequences projecting ever onwards. What sets the beginning and end of an argument is not, therefore, the concept of discourse itself, but some real empirical factor: the contingent human will or convenience that drives the production of this or that discourse in particular.

This empirical factor is simply the desire for *maximum certainty* or *the inconvenience of sufficing with minimum certainty*; otherwise put, the desire to extend the credibility of the known to the knowable. In each argument, individually considered, a human decision clips the y-axis that is the scale of credibility and draws out the x-axis of a second polarity: in each concrete case, *maximum certainty is not always possible, and minimum certainty is not always enough for the desired ends.* Out of this, we derive two intermediary forms of discourse. *Note bene: two* types, not one, as would be the case with a simple point on a vertical scale. These two points, or intermediary types, are, on one hand, the discourse that *tends toward a maximum certainty it cannot reach*, and, on the other, that which neither needs nor aspires to maximum certainty, *but can obtain something a little sturdier than minimum certainty.* So, between the discourse that bases itself upon that which is absolutely true and that which grounds itself in the merely possible, we find two intermediary discourses that are not points on a linear scale, but movements, tensions, dynamisms that strike out, laterally, from a maximum point toward a minimum, or from a minimum to a maximum, as follows:

MAXIMUM
(certain, true)

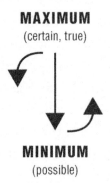

MINIMUM
(possible)

The former is that which embarks from sufficient credibility, that is, from the *probable*; and the latter is that which, unable to attain to truth, or even to the probable, nevertheless refuses to settle for the merely possible, and pursues the *likely*.

For Aristotle, there are four levels of veracity: the

certain, the *probable*, the *likely*, and the *possible*. Corresponding to those levels are the four types of propositions and the degrees of credibility to which they can aspire in their conclusions. An argument can only claim a level of belief that is commensurate with the credibility of its premises; if the starting point of the argument is a merely possible premise, its conclusions can be possible at best. If it sets out from a premise assumed to be absolutely certain, it can presume to arrive at absolutely certain conclusions. This is the universal, *a priori* foundation of the four discourses addressed in Aristotle's *Organon*:

1. *Analytical discourse*—formal logic—is that which builds from premises that are taken as absolutely certain or universally accepted, and it proceeds in accordance with a rigorous set of formal laws of thought (syllogistic logic) until it arrives at absolutely certain or universally undeniable conclusions.

2. *Dialectical discourse* is that which embarks from premises that could be uncertain, but which are accepted under certain circumstances by a more or less homogeneous public that is knowledgeable in the matter in hand. In other words, its premises are *probably true*. Dialectical discourse accepts varying lines of possible development for these premises, which it then compares and contrasts, excluding some and combining others in accordance with the rules of logical coherency.

3. *Rhetorical discourse* takes as its starting point the current convictions (whether true or false) of the general populace and seeks to guide the audience toward a *likely* conclusion.

4. *Poetic discourse* works with the public's taste and

habitual mental/imaginative repertoires. Playing with the possibilities it encounters therein, it tries to create an appearance or simulacrum with which it can lure the audience/public into temporarily and voluntarily engaging with something it knows to be mere fiction or artistic convention as if it were factually true.

FINAL SCHEMA FOR THE UNIVERSAL TYPOLOGY OF DISCOURSES

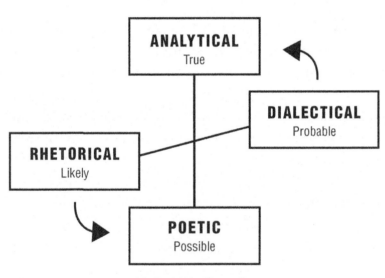

Vertical Axis: Necessity
Transversal Axis: Contingency

5. The Conditions of Credibility

W E HAVE SEEN THAT the four discourses differ mainly in their respective degrees and modes of credibility. Now we will study in greater detail the psychological reasons that determine that credibility in each of the four cases.

I. Poetic Discourse

The credibility of poetic discourse derives from its *magic*, which makes the listener "participate" in a world of perceptions, evocations, and feelings. As there is no distance between the poet and her public, the result is a spiritual and contemplative communion of experiences "as if life itself were speaking" (as a reviewer said of Tolstoy, though it holds just as well for poets in general). It was based on this that Samuel Taylor Coleridge said that one of the basic conditions for the appreciation of poetry is "suspension of disbelief"; suspension of doubt and realist critical demands. The listener or reader of the poetic work provisionally "brackets out" all critical judgement so that he or she might participate more directly in the contemplative experience proposed by the poet. The analogy between contemplation of art and the phenomenological ἐποχή (epoché) is clear here: in both cases, we suspend the customary judgements of "existence" so as to better apprehend "essences".

In poetic discourse, credibility therefore becomes a sort of *willing participation in the contemplative experience* the poet proposes.

Another precondition of the "magical" effect of this participation is a community of language between poet and listener; they must not only speak the same language, but possess a commensurate mastery of its vocabulary, syntax, etc. For the poetic effect to flourish, what the poet says must be immediately grasped, without unnecessary intellectual mediations. But there is, naturally, a difference here: the poet's mastery of the resources of language must be *active*—in the sense of affording the capacity to use that language creatively—while the reader's or listener's need only be *passive*—sufficient to understand usage he or she might not necessarily be able to produce with similar effect.

This is the reason why poetic works produced in the distant past, crafted with antiquated vocabulary or with structures and turns of phrase that strike us as odd today, no longer have the same poetic effect unless the language barrier can be artificially removed through philological intervention or glossing, or some personal effort of research, analysis and interpretation. Aesthetic appreciation of ancient or arcane works is an indirect experience garnered through intellectual and critical mediation. And as, for the average man and woman in the street, intellectual and critical activity is separated from direct experience by a yawning gulf that only lengthy education can bridge, such mediation is, in practice, inaccessible to the vast majority. The possibility of "recovering" the archetypal, living meaning of poetic experience depends on the audience's level of culture and capacity: the better versed a reader is in technical interpretive procedures, the less grueling the required intellectual mediation will be, and the more readily accessible the poetic experience will become. For the beginner, the hard work that goes into interpretation is an obstacle that closes the doors onto poetic worlds. The habitual study of philology and constant exercise of interpretation opens horizons which the common reader could never even dream exist.

Of course, there are exceptions, works which, though written in bygone times, remain (more or less) directly accessible without posing greater difficulties in terms of interpretation. In many cases this apparent ease is deceptive, based on fortuitous affinities. Modern readers will often end up appreciating a work for reasons that have nothing really to do with it. Those familiar with psychoanalytical ideas, for example, may value *Oedipus Rex* without noting that Sophocles' Oedipus did not actually suffer from the Freudian complex that bears his name. Likewise, young people thirsty for "mystical experience" beyond the customary "dogma" they consider too strict will babble with admiration for Saint John of the Cross without realizing that it is impossible to truly understand

Saint John of the Cross outside the Catholic dogma they eschew. It's like a Brazilian Indian arriving in São Paulo or Rio de Janeiro and seeing the statues of Peri and Ceci in the public squares,[1] only to develop the wildly mistaken idea that the indigenous tribes were objects of worship in the big cities. Or, to give a more comic example, they are like the Baron of Itararé,[2] who joined the Integralist movement because he'd misread the slogan as "Adeus, Patria e Família" ("goodbye, homeland and family"), not "Deus, Patria e Familia" ("God, homeland and family").

Only genuine literary culture can cure such subjective misconceptions, which seem to me to be the standard for literary taste among today's university students. Their literary education, based upon the occasional cult to authors picked willy-nilly—or after the preferences of their teachers or the whims of fashion—does not afford them a rounded view of the literary world on any level, historically or in terms of a hierarchy of values, or as a system of genres and forms, such that their literary taste ends up repeating the parable of the blind men and the elephant. It's a pillar, said the first, feeling the animal's leg; no, it's a snake, said the second, feeling its trunk. Not at all, it's a banana tree, said the third, mistaking the ear for a leaf. As a result of experiences of this sort, the youth of today, armed with a few years of "study", conclude that arbitrary taste is, on such matters, the gold standard of judgment. It's a flattering conclusion, because, in our times of narcissism and the cult of youth, everybody under the age of thirty is just dying to become—him or herself—the very measure of all things. The result is a horde of illiterate mini-tyrants.

True literary culture can correct these distortions by infusing the experience of the poetic work with a sense of proportion, appropriateness of meaning, hierarchy and literary values, etc.

In any case, first impressions of affinity and private agreement should never be taken as criteria for a value judgement. There may be works that don't "speak" to us directly, but which might nonetheless have a lot to say once we learn to understand them. Opening ourselves up to new possibilities of understanding is the essence of education. But philology is not just about building bridges. It's also about blowing up false bridges and restoring that alien feeling when it is preferable to a facile, illusory connection with a work: recognizing that we don't fully understand something is often the first step towards genuine comprehension. That's why there is nothing that grates an educator more than youngsters who cling to their own opinions like curmudgeonly old men, entrenched, wary and hostile, behind their barricades.

Another potential misunderstanding to be rectified out of hand is that the "communion of experiences" to which I referred earlier is not directly sensory or emotive, but spiritual and contemplative. As Carlos Bousoño notes, when the poet describes a toothache, the description does not hurt the reader in the teeth: proof that we're dealing with the contemplation of experiences, not actual experiences themselves. The warning is unnecessary to those who have understood from the start that all four discourses are directed to the spirit (to humans as thinking beings capable of reflecting upon lived experience), but it becomes essential when we consider that failure to grasp this indirect, representative character of discourse is the general rule among younger readers, who demand direct and facile emotions from works of literature, without any aesthetic mediation. It's a misunderstanding that conflates art with life, without realizing that, by so doing, they end up cultivating a repetitive, narcotic art that is "reactionary" in the sense of blocking access to any experience that does not already lie within the reader's preferred and habitual circle of references.

What was said about community of language, on the other hand, should not be mistaken to mean that a work of art can only move us if written in the vernacular, limited to current usage. On the contrary, in fact. If common usage itself had the power to move us, we would spend our lives immersed in an ocean of emotions and never once lapse into banality or boredom. Poetic discourse works because it is "strange" enough to break through boredom and banality. But there are two types of "strangeness": the magical, which bewitches, and the intellectual, which alienates. Intellectual alienation puts a critical distance between the reader and the poetic work that weakens or nullifies the poetic experience; while the sense of magical strangeness invests poetic language with an aura of prestige and oracular authority that catapults it into the realm which the romantics called "the sublime", beyond the merely "beautiful". The difference is that one of these senses of strangeness holds the work aloof, at odds, while the other absorbs us through fascination and participation. This is not the place to examine in detail how these effects are produced. (Brechtian "alienation effect", which falls under the intellectual kind of strangeness, is something quite apart. To prevent any confusion: Bertolt Brecht's plays cause the audience to experience a very specific critical alienation with respect to the characters' actions within the work, but not toward the work itself. In this sense, behind the curtain of critical distancing, it retains its powerful "magical" influence.) For the time being, what interests us here is to show that the credibility of poetic discourse derives from the "magic" conjured by the listener's willing participation in a contemplative experience, and that this consent takes the form of a suspension of disbelief, a (provisional and commitment-free) agreement to "play along".

Finally, this community of experience should be understood in the spiritual and contemplative sense, not physical, as it should not be seen as something limited to the "subjective" sphere of experience. Nothing excludes the hypothesis that, by spiritual means, the poetic product can literally work "physical" effects upon the reader, and that these effects are not objective or replicable under the right cultural and psychological conditions. Indeed, in the earliest times of human culture, poetic language was recognized as wielding precisely this power, the ability to trigger physical effects on nature by the magic of words alone. The shared origins of poetry and magic (understood as the science and technique of working with the subtle forces of nature) pose a particularly thorny and complex problem which we will address more carefully further on. For now, it is enough merely to show that poetic experience is not by any means dependent on pure subjective randomness and that, the initial conditions withstanding, that is, willingness to participate and a community of linguistic resources, the poetic effect plays itself out along perfectly identifiable lines. It is, therefore, a matter of science, and not in the least arbitrary.

II. Rhetorical Discourse

Rhetorical discourse is essentially designed to persuade someone to do, or refrain from doing, something specific: approve or reject a law; declare war or establish peace; elect or overthrow a ruler; absolve or condemn a defendant. All rhetorical discourse contains, with varying degrees of explicitness, a command or an appeal. Its goal is to ensure the appeal is accepted or the command obeyed.

The argument's influence over the listener is therefore very different from that exercised by poetic discourse, which strives to bring about a transformation in the listener's soul. However, as that change is brought in the deeper recesses of our being, it cannot trigger an immediate external and practical effect, such as spurring a specific action or decision. In fact, poetic discourse suggests from afar rather than commands or exhorts in the here-and-now. Rhetorical discourse, on the other hand, does not run as deep as the poetic, but is more evident and immediate, more translatable into external action. While poetic discourse attempts to seep into the listener's soul, leaving a deep mark that becomes part and parcel of his or her personality "as if life itself were speaking", and for that very reason refrains from drawing any direct or present benefit, rhetorical discourse is content to influence the listener for a given period towards specific ends, such as a particular action or decision. The attorney or barrister addressing the court has no interest in working any deep or lasting changes upon the jurors' souls, merely to persuade them to acquit or condemn the defendant in the dock. The lawyer doesn't care if they regret the decision later. The shelf life of rhetorical discourse is short and ends as soon as the desired effect is obtained.

Poetic discourse plants the seeds of future conduct but gives no orders. Even when it expresses commandments, as in the case of religious epics, it does so through a symbolic language that is open to a world of later interpretations, and it is only through those interpretations (which are themselves expressed, in turn, in rhetorical or dialectical language) that the commandments—general by nature—become determinant norms. However, some sacred texts contain exhortations and explicit commands mixed amongst the symbolic expressions. Hence some scholars, such as Frye, prefer to classify those apart, in an intermediary genre called *Kerygma*, a fusion of the poetic and rhetorical. It's a valid enough denomination, so long as we bear in mind that the poetic and rhetorical elements of a discourse never form a homogeneous blend but are always distinguishable one from the other.

Rhetorical discourse, for its part, always issues an order or appeal that, even when only implicit, is never anything less than concrete and targeted, and that is why it must always be literal and readily intelligible (that is, it must refer directly to the practical circumstances in play). Poetic discourse is open to multiple "interpretations" (as many as there are interpreters) without that in any way diminishing its effect, which, if anything, will be magnified by the depth these layers of meaning bring. Rhetorical discourse, on the other hand, has to be unequivocal. Rhetoric that is open to interpretation fails as rhetoric. Obtuse or obscure words might fascinate and move, but they will not transmit a clear order. (Though this does not mean to say that rhetorical discourse is devoid of all poetic flair, or that its literal message, once guaranteed, cannot be regaled with symbolic meanings).

The credibility of rhetorical discourse consists in its power to persuade or urge someone to action (either in support of or opposition to its underlying cause). It's an effect obtained through an apparent and temporary identification of the listener's will with that of the orator. Rhetoric makes listeners feel that the argument laid out coincides with their innermost beliefs. So we are no longer talking about a willing participation in a certain contemplative experience here, but the open admission of a shared will. In other words, a decision.

Deep down, rhetorical discourse appeals to the listener's sense of freedom, to the impulse to decide, to act for oneself, to assert one's own will. That's why it was so important in the rhetoric of old that the orator first read the crowd, as it were, to build the needed bridge between the general opinion and the desired objective.

Of course, some such bridges are false: the skilled but unscrupulous orator can make the auditorium believe that they want the same thing, when in fact they want different things, even if they are made to forget that for a time. However, the efficiency of such trickery is limited, and its constant use serves only to diminish the speaker's credibility. True rhetoric is always based on the authentic will of the audience, which it strives only to steer or gently shape, without forcing changes or hoodwinking the listeners. Abraham Lincoln, one of the greatest orators who ever lived, once said that "You can fool some of the people some of the time, but you can't fool all of the people all of the time." True rhetoric knows that the audience can only be persuaded to do what it actually wants and that the best it can aim for is to swap a superficial, momentary will for another, deeper drive already latent somewhere in the heart. As such, rhetoric appeals to what is best in the listener's soul, and that is what gives it its moral and political function, as an exercise in responsible decision-making.

III. Dialectical Discourse

Dialectical discourse endeavors to convince the listener through reasoning alone, irrespective of his or her will, and sometimes even contrary to it. To make that possible, the sole precondition is that the listener must acquiesce to the arbitration of reason and accept certain shared premises, usually drawn from beliefs currently held within the social and cultural world at large or from scientific consensus.

Note how, in the scale of discourses, there is a steady decline in the credence the discourse is initially given. Poetic discourse required suspension of disbelief, which means little or no resistance at all; while rhetorical discourse required a certain trust or sympathy toward the person of the orator (essential dispositions that must be won if not immediately forthcoming). Dialectical discourse asks much less of its listeners, merely that they trust in their own powers of reasoning and in some generally-accepted premises. The manner in which the argument progresses will be controlled by the listener themself, who can reject any conclusions that don't seem to follow logically.

The credibility of dialectical discourse depends, therefore, solely on these two factors:

1. The listener has to agree to follow the logic of the argument and accept as true any conclusions that follow logically upon the premises and which cannot be refuted by logical means.

2. The argument must embark from mutually accepted premises, taken as initial common ground.

This credibility therefore depends on the listener's level of cultural development (ability to follow the argument) and intellectual honesty (willingness to accept conclusions they cannot refute). As such, dialectical discourse requires a rational and reasonable interlocutor whose knowledge repertoire overlaps to some degree with that of the speaker; who agrees to conduct the debate in a rational and reasonable way; and is willing to accept the stronger argument. The success of dialectical debate hinges on these conditions and these alone.

IV. Analytical Discourse

Starting out from premises that are taken as evident and unquestionable, and aiming to achieve results that should be accepted as absolutely certain, the credibility of analytical discourse depends on two things: that listeners are capable of accompanying the progression of the argument step-by-step, without missing a beat, and that they are in agreement with the absolute veracity of the starting premises. The first of these conditions requires specialist training in logic. The second can only hold in two cases: (a) when the premises are so general that no one of sound mind could possibly doubt them (an example would be the principle of non-contradiction); or (b) when the discourse is directed toward an informed scientific public knowledgeable enough to be able to take specific premises drawn from some sector of science as absolutely certain, either because they have the tools at hand to verify them scientifically or because they are skilled in dealing with admittedly relative premises by abstracting that relativity and agreeing, through scientific convention, to accept them provisionally as absolute and setting aside anything that might challenge them. Otherwise put, analytical discourse can only function when discussing very general truths with a very general public, or specific truths with a specialist public.

For example, a group of physicists might agree by convention that certain principles of physics are unassailably true, despite knowing that any or all of those truths may well be debunked tomorrow or next week. For the time being, however, they continue to take them as valid until proven otherwise, despite making every effort to disprove them themselves. This mental attitude, which blends the absolute logical rigor of conclusions with an understanding of the permanent revocability of the premises, is a prominent characteristic of the scientific spirit and can prove extremely uncomfortable for the listener, even the cultured listener who lacks specialist training. The credibility of analytical discourse depends on the scientific capacity of the audience. Here it is worth recalling the warning given by Saint Albert the Great that for most people, "accustomed to vulgarity and ignorance, philosophical certainty appears arid and sad, either because, not having studied it, they are unable to understand the language, and are unfamiliar with the efficacy of the syllogistic apparatus, or through their own lack of reason or skill. Effectively, a truth obtained by syllogistic means is such that the unstudied cannot readily attain to it, whilst it lies altogether beyond the reach of the short-sighted".[3]

6. Milestones in the History of Aristotelian Studies in the West

THE HISTORY OF Aristotelian studies in the West unfolded out of multiple notable discoveries that have periodically brought new aspects of the Stagirite's work to light.

In the 1st Century BCE, the revelation of Aristotle's writings as found and edited by Andronicus of Rhodes signaled the beginning Aristotelian studies.

In the 6th Century CE, Boethius' translation of Aristotle's works on logic saw his thought begin to be absorbed by the Church, a process that would reach its height with Saint Thomas Aquinas in the 13th Century. It is on the strength of this contribution that Boethius is considered the first scholastic. Before him, Aristotle was by no means unknown, but he was understood in very generic terms, largely conflated with the Platonists under the wider designation of "the Academy".

In the *Commentaries* on Aristotle by Saints Albert the

Great and Thomas Aquinas (13th Century), the West was finally gifted a complete and structured vision of Aristotle's thought, previously known only in partial and fragmented form.

Aristotle's *Poetics,* lost since Antiquity, was rediscovered in the 16th Century. The commented edition by Francesco Robortelli caused frissons throughout educated Europe and effectively shaped the literary aesthetic of classicism, which would dominate Western literature until the 18th Century.[1]

In the 19th Century, the standard edition of Aristotle's writings, published by the Academy of Berlin under the editorship of Immanuel Bekker, escalated interest in Aristotelian studies. As a result, the systemic vision of Aristotle's philosophy that began with the scholastics was perfected and confirmed in a series of notable volumes, particularly Félix Ravaisson's *Essay on Aristotle's Metaphysics* (1837), Franz Brentano's *On the Several Senses of Being in Aristotle* (1862), and Octave Hamelin's *Le Systeme d'Aristote* (a course administered in 1904-5 and published posthumously by Léon Robin, in 1920).

At the turn of the 20th Century, this systemic vision was contested by Werner Jaeger (*Aristotle: Fundamentals of the History of His Development,* 1923). According to Jaeger, founder of the so-called "genetic" school, Aristotle started out as a pure Platonic metaphysician and ended up a "positive" natural scientist, averse to metaphysics. Jaeger's position was radicalized by Pierre Aubenque (*The Problem of Being in Aristotle,* 1962), who painted a tragic, almost skeptical Aristotle in opposition to Platonic religiosity.

In response to all this, Ingemar Düring (*Aristotle's Protrepticus: An Attempt at Reconstruction*, 1961) explored Aristotle's earlier writings and concluded in favor of the genetic method, while rejecting Jaeger's thesis of a radical shift in orientation in the Greek's later output. In parallel, Augustin Mansion (*Philosophie première, philosophie seconde et métaphysique chez Aristote*, 1958) and Eugenio Berti (*A Unidade do Saber em Aristótles*, 1965) rejected the latter part of Jaeger's theses by showing that, in Aristotle, Physics is inseparable from Metaphysics.

In the 1950s, an entirely new line of investigation was introduced by Eric Weil (*The Place of Logic in Aristotle's Thought*, 1951), who proposed the revolutionary thesis that dialectic, not logic, is the true scientific method in Aristotle. The thesis was demonstrated in detail by Jean-Paul Dumont in his *Introduction a la Methode d'Aristote* (1986). Against both Jaeger and Aubenque, Dumont made a decisive contribution towards proving the unity of the Aristotelian system.

Of course, there have been hundreds if not thousands of other noteworthy works. But the eight mentioned above laid the milestones that marked the watersheds of substantial change in the way Aristotle was understood and absorbed in the West.

My own work consciously seeks insertion in this evolutionary arc,[2] drawing upon the contributions of Weil and Dumont to lay out a much more systemic, cohesive and "organic" vision of Aristotle than even the scholastics could have imagined.

Weil conjectured that a new approach to Aristotle's

method would create an about-turn in the way his philosophy is viewed as a whole. This new approach would begin with a question (so obvious that nobody had ever thought to ask it over the course of twenty centuries): *if logic is so central to Aristotle, why doesn't he use it in his treatises, instead of dialectical exposition?*

Expanding upon Weil's hypothesis, Dumont meticulously demonstrated that "those who cleave to the shallow interpretation of Aristotle that reduces the *Topics* [i.e., the Dialectic] to a mere introductory discourse to the *Posterior Analytics* [i.e., the Logic] likewise reduce Aristotelianism to an attempt to found a pure logical formalism—a very frequent mistake, as it happens. [In so doing], they prevent us from recognizing the creative power and ingenious depth of the *Topics*, the work of a young philosopher *already in possession of an original method*. Aristotle's method lays the groundwork for a metaphysics that is equipped to confront the complementary viewpoints that express the diversity of causes".[3]

Before looking at Dumont's work, but already convinced of the Weilian conclusions he would go on to confirm, I found myself pondering the following issues:

I. If Aristotle already possessed a complete dialectical method since his youth, then he must have created it during the years he was teaching Rhetoric at the Academy. Rather than one following upon the other, his Rhetoric and Dialectic were therefore developed at the same time, and in close association. Aristotle sees his Dialectic as a theoretical deepening of the Rhetoric, and his Rhetoric as a "political" expression of the Dialectic. In this case, the separation later forced upon the *Topics* and

Rhetoric by Andronicus of Rhodes has editorial arrangement value only and does not reflect the close lineage these sciences share in Aristotle's wider vision.

2. Weil is entirely right in stressing the importance of the *Topics*, the relegation of which, as Dumont saw so clearly, would transform Aristotelianism into "a pure logical formalism" contrary to the philosopher's own express intentions. We should not forget that, for Aristotle, logic discovers nothing, it simply confirms what has been discovered by other means. However, merely stating that is not enough. Aristotle would allow no separation, no gulf between logical formalism and concrete experience; a separation that would foster a knowledge that is logically correct, but ontologically false. Hence his thinly veiled disdain for mathematicians, math being a study he considered good for teenagers but little else. However, in this case, in order to save his system from such an ungrounded formalism, there must be, within the Aristotelian method itself, some bridge between discursive thought and sense data.

3. Where is this bridge? It is not in the *Topics*, because dialectic does not deal with immediate data but with prevailing scientific consensus. It must therefore lie at a more primary level. But it's not in the *Rhetoric* either, because rhetorical argumentation is not founded upon sense data, but on commonly held beliefs.

4. Of all philosophers, Aristotle is the one who most vehemently stressed the systemic unity of knowledge. As such, there would be no sense whatsoever in his employing a stolid two-story method—discourse on top, the senses below, as in some *avant la lettre* Cartesianism.

On the contrary: to ensure the bare minimum of coherency for Aristotelianism, there had to be a rigorous homology between the structure of his method and the global structure of Aristotelian science; a science that originates in individual sentient beings, gradually elevates through species and genera, and finally obtains to universal being. The cognitive bridge between concrete sentient beings and abstract species is, according to Aristotle, *phantasia* (a function that encompasses both memory and imagination). *Phantasia*, as a real phenomenon, is studied in the treatise *De Anima* (psychology). So, to complete the overlap between the method and the system of science, we still need that part of the method that corresponds to psychology in the sciences, and that studies the method by which, starting out from sensory data, the psyche forms the images (*phantasmata*) that will ground our concepts of species. No such part exists in the Aristotelian corpus as it survives today, though mention is made of it in the *Poetics*. For Aristotle, poetry acts upon the human body through sound and image (in theater), and, by presenting us with universal truths through the characters' actions, it functions in a manner precisely analogous to *phantasia*, in which the image of a body in space can represent not just one single being, but all beings of that species, therefore bridging the gap between perception and thought. As such, in the sphere of method—that is, of the sciences of discourse— Poetics corresponds to that "first floor", the connection between sense data and the universe of discourse. Poetry is the bridge between "world" and "discourse". Without poetics, understood as the seed of the discursive method, Aristotelianism is cut off from that material and sensible root that was so important to the Stagirite, and drove his precocious rupture with the Platonic doctrine of the Forms.

Based upon these grounds, my thesis demonstrates in a far more radical manner even than Weil and Dumont the deep-run unity of inspiration that presides over Aristotle's entire *oeuvre*. It heads off at every turn any attempt to transform Aristotelianism into the instrument of a tragic dualism, materialism or mathematizing Neo-Platonism. It takes Aristotle's thesis of the unity of knowledge to its logical conclusion, showing that this unity cannot be wholly fulfilled on the level of discourse, but requires the rooting of discourse in the sensory world, biological life and the social context. For Aristotle, discourse does not form a world apart, but pertains to a living thing's natural, "biological" drive to elevate itself to the universal conception that includes it.

My thesis looks to recover the "systemic" and "ecological" spirit of Aristotelianism at a time when universal culture is so anxiously striving to restore the systemic and unitary meaning of knowledge and integrate it with an ecological—or eco-cosmic—vision of the living being. This need is eloquently expressed by Edgar Morin:

> I am increasingly convinced that anthroposocial science must be articulated with the science of nature, and that this articulation requires a reorganization of the structure of knowledge itself.4

Aristotle in a New Perspective

Taking into account that Aristotle is one of the founding fathers of Western culture and science and the inventor of the very notion of a "structure of knowledge", what could be more important to the contemporary scientific debate than to rediscover in his work the root of that integrative and systemic spirit of which Morin speaks?

7. Notes on a Possible Conclusion

T HE IDEA OF the Four Discourses is not expounded in any of Aristotle's writings, but it nonetheless pervades his thought as a whole and underlies not only his treatises on Physics, Metaphysics, Ethics and Politics, but also his typical *modus exponendi et argumentandi.*[1]

It is in this idea, not the explicit content of the theses defended in each stage of Aristotle's intellectual development, that we should seek the key to the philosopher's system. As I see it, it's quite odd that anyone might think it possible to contest this unity through recourse to biographical considerations—highly conjectural I might add—because in Aristotelianism, like any other philosophy or indeed human endeavor, the final unity cannot be achieved in the domain of production *per se* but remains forever a guiding ideal that only appears *as such* before the beginning and after the end.

That the end pursued by Aristotle's philosophy (to constitute knowledge as a demonstrative and apodeictic system) remained forever only an ideal is something evinced by the fact that not one of the master's known treatises employs logical demonstration rather than dialectical argumentation as its method. If we accept, in light of the *Theory of the Four Discourses*, that for Aristotle knowledge is like a tree whose roots penetrate the soil of sensations as it rises upwards, through imagination, will and thought, into the apodeictic heights of certainty, we must also admit that the life of human knowledge can never be cut off from those roots through encapsulation within a demonstrative system without that system limiting itself, by that very act, to only the most general and abstract planes within the sphere of known things. A system of that kind could never yield effective knowledge of anything, as it would merely be a formula for a possible knowledge which only a return to the individual things and beings presented to us by the senses could make real. In the Aristotelian sense, the sage is not someone who has ascended to the heavens of Platonic forms, but someone who, upon returning from those heights, knows how to *recognize* the principle of unity latent within the variety of sensible things presented to them in space and time. Aristotelian wisdom is not just *episteme* (intellectually certain knowledge), but *phronesis* (prudence), the wisdom to act, the inner voice that guides the soul through the shadows of life and its ever-changing situations. Bringing the demonstrative system to complete fruition would dispense with *phronesis*, because it would turn us all into gods or angels.

The debate between those who see Aristotle as *systematic* and those who consider him *aporetic* (proceeding philosophically by agency of doubt or puzzlement) is therefore resolved in an Aristotle who cyclically rises into the unity of system through *aporetic* means (dialectic) only to return to the variety of problematic experience guided by the memory of that unity, a light that is none other than *phronesis*, our lodestar in both scientific investigation and active life.

It is in this dynamic circularity (rather than the pure and simple architecture of the actual theses) that we find the essential unity of the Aristotelian system, not a simple unity, but a unity of the diverse, as in everything that is real and living. Moreover, it is a unity that is defined by an *entelechy* (fully realized actuality) as opposed to a simple, more or less mechanical logical coherency between the parts, or a utopian and quite unnecessary persistence of the same convictions over a lifetime; because this unity is never—in all living things, and especially so in the living thing called humankind—a static equivalence of all moments. Rather it is the striving, through diversity, toward a finality that encompasses, explains and redeems all.

We must never forget that when Aristotle joined the Academy he brought with him a vast knowledge of anatomy and physiology acquired within the home, and that this knowledge had already deeply instilled in him a notion of *organicity*, or of *unity through the diverse*, which would guide all of his logical, physical, metaphysical and ethical speculations moving forward and become the unmistakable hallmark of his style of thinking.

In his early investigations on the theory of discourse, recorded in *The Categories*, we already see Aristotle wrestling with the problem of the various senses of being. It is actually quite staggering that modern Aristotle scholars attribute the philosopher's solution to the problem to purely grammatical and linguistic specula- tions,[2] rather than look for the young philosopher's inspi- ration in the simple experience of the unity of the diverse carried over from his learning as a physician's son (his father, Nicomachus, was the private physician to King Amyntas of Macedon).

After describing the system of the categories from a purely logical and linguistic perspective, that is as a simple classification of possible predicates (he lists ten: substance, quantity, quality, relation, place, time, position, doing, having, and being affected), Jonathan Barnes asks:[3] "Why the shift from classes of predicates to classes of beings?" It's an odd question, as this "shift", this change, only exists for Barnes and modern interpreters in general, accustomed as they are to taking the logical/linguistic perspective as prior and independent. Not so for Aristotle, for whom knowledge does not follow the models of language, but rather language presents itself from the outset after the organic model of the unity of the diverse —a model Aristotle already knew. The system of cate- gories is a biological approach to language and thought, not a logico-linguistic approach to knowledge.

So much so that unity in the diverse is the key with which Aristotle strives to solve every problem he comes across: from issues of method (such as the famous dialec- tical resolutions according to the different meanings of the same word)[4] to those of physics (the different perspectives that enable one to address the soul, for example), and even the supreme questions of metaphysics.[5]

Now, the unity of the diverse, as the supreme key, cannot itself be explained and grounded: it seems to be, for Aristotle, one of those basal truths that require no proof, even if, as Dumont showed, it provided the foundation for the very principle of the dialectical method that would, in turn, lead to the revelation of the first principles of the analytics.

If we ask where the young Aristotle discovered this supreme principle, there is only one answer: in his contemplation of living organisms.

At the Academy, however, Aristotle would acquire a notion that, once blended with the unity of the diverse, gave rise to the theory of the Four Discourses, the creation of the Aristotelian method as a whole, and the young philosopher's definitive appropriation of his special spiritual powers.

It's a notion which Plato conveyed through his Analogy of the Divided Line.[6] The diagram is presented in *The Republic*, Plato's mature work, and we can suppose it was teaching material and subject for debate at the Academy at around the time the young Aristotle was studying there, and upon whom it must have left quite an impression—the fertile kind which he attributes to the mysteries and their rites.

Aristotle in a New Perspective

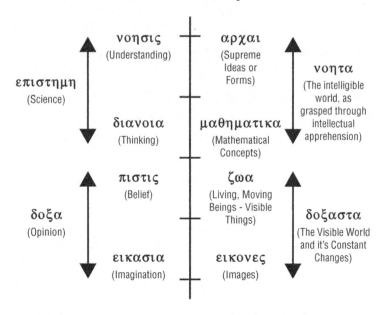

On the far left, bottom to top, the first column reads: *doxa* (opinion) and *episteme* (science), i.e., the lower and higher forms of knowledge. On the far right, we have the respective objects of these modalities: *doxasta* (the visible world and its constant changes) and *noeta* (the intelligible world, as grasped through intellectual apprehension). Next column in from the left we have the cognitive faculties, two pertaining to opinion—*eikasia* (imagination) and *pistis* (belief)—and two related to knowledge—*dianoia* (thinking) and *noesis* (understanding). Again, these form an ascending scale. Next over, we have the objects of knowledge corresponding to these faculties: *eikones* (images); *zoa* (living, moving beings—visible things); *mathematika* (mathematical concepts); and, lastly, *Arkhai*, the supreme ideas or Forms.

Plato does not give precise explanations or definitions for any of these concepts, but it is clear that the schema presents the framework of the Platonic gnoseology. It is also evident that there is a rigid correspondence between the four faculties in the center-left column and the four discourses of Aristotle:

FACULTY (Plato)	DISCOURSE (Aristotle)
Eikasia (Imagination)	Poetics
Pistis (Belief)	Rhetoric
Dianoia (Thought)	Dialectic
Noesis (Understanding)	Analytics

Elementary prudence would recommend that we see in this Platonic schema the origin of the concepts of the Four Discourses and the schematization of the respective sciences in Aristotle.

Even more interesting, however, is to observe that there is no exact symmetrical correspondence between the objects Plato specifies for the four faculties (in the center-right column) and the objects of the four discourses, with their ascending scale from the poetic to the analytical. Whereas images are the object of poetic discourse, living beings are not the object of rhetoric, but of dialectic, which, for Aristotle, is the method proper to physics; mathematical concepts, for their part, are the objects of apodeictic demonstration, not dialectical dispute; while, finally, the *arkhai* or supreme Forms, are not, for Aristotle, objects of any discourse at all, but of self-evident intuitive knowledge (which one arrives at through dialectic).

Both the symmetry and asymmetry we find here show that Aristotle was deeply influenced by the Platonic scale of the modalities of knowledge (to the point of preserving it in his four discourses), and yet, in an attempt to lend these modalities a rigorous conceptualization he found lacking in Platonism, and hoping, at the same time, to confer an organic coherency after his own style of thinking, he found himself obliged to break the symmetry of the Platonic model and impose a different direction upon his own gnoseological speculations. This is a constant in Aristotle's philosophical development: conserving Platonism here, surpassing it there.

It's no coincidence that the top of the scale is the most intriguing part of the comparison between the Platonic and Aristotelian schemas. If, in Platonism, supreme knowledge, *noesis*, gives us knowledge of the *arkhai* or Forms, and if, in Aristotelianism, the supreme discourse, the analytical, does not give us any knowledge at all, properly speaking, but merely apodeictic certainty of knowledge already obtained, then we see inferred in Aristotle the ideal of a knowledge in which fully-realized analytical discourse coincides with the self-evidence of the *arkhai* grasped by intellectual intuition, a knowledge in which full probatory capacity is equivalent to the plenitude of intuitive evidence. Otherwise put, the supreme ideal of knowledge includes at once, in an indissoluble synthesis, the immediate evidence of intuition and the persuasiveness of rational proof. Only the complete fulfillment of this ideal would allow knowledge to be truly systematic, without any aporetic residue. But it is an ideal that can be neither attained nor abandoned. It cannot be attained because its full fruition across all domains of knowledge would be equivalent to the quantitative infinite in actuality, something Aristotle himself shows to be impossible. Nor can it be abandoned, because it is the image of infinite (not quantitative) knowledge that drives and structures the attainment of possible wisdom, without which we would be lost to an empiricism bereft of rational structure and all apodeictic foundation.[7]

That is why Aristotle is at once a systematic and aporetic thinker; that's why, guiding himself by the ideal of the logico-analytical system, he proceeds, in practice, through the dialectical method; that is why, with an eye on the universal and eternal, he insists on pursuing it in the here and now, in the particular entities of the visible world; that is why he proclaims—and in apparent contradiction—that the supreme reality is God and that the only reality that exists is that of individual sensible things in general and of living beings in particular; that is why, of all the Greek philosophers, Aristotle would become the master of choice for later Christian thinkers: because, through the enigma of the *universal in the living singular*, his thought foreshadowed the mystery of the Incarnation. Active devotion to supreme science and infinite wisdom is, in the final analysis, the essence of all true philosophy and true religion.

Aristotle at the Dentist: A Polemic Between the Author and the SPBC

I. De re Aristotelica Opiniones Abominandae: The Dead Cat's Meow

Depressing considerations on the "Critical Assessment" of my work An Aristotelian Philosophy of Culture *by the Editorial Committee of* Ciência Hoje *magazine, run by the Brazilian Society for the Progress of Science (SBPC).*

Backstory — Toward the end of 1993, my work "An Aristotelian Philosophy of Culture", the framework of some classes I was giving on "The Thought and Present Relevance of Aristotle" at the Laura Alvim House of Culture, was submitted to *Ciência Hoje* magazine by Dr. Ivan da Costa Marques, a member of that society who, I am honored to say, was frequenting my course.

When almost a year passed without response, I felt at liberty to publish the article in a book. At the start of October 1994, I received the first impeccably rendered copies from the printers. That same day — mere coincidence or Jungian synchronicity I cannot say — I found an envelope on my doorstep from the SBPC, returning the originals with a rejection letter saying that, as the paper was on *education in odontology* (yes, that was the word used: odontology), I would be better served placing it in a specialist publication.

So I wrote back saying that neither I nor Aristotle ever suspected this hidden inclination towards dentistry in our speculations; that the return of the pages was not only late, but unnecessary, seeing as the work was just about to come out in a book; and that, in light of the sheer oddness of the reason given for declining the piece, it seemed likely that the submission had not been examined at all.

Some days later, I received a testy letter from the editor, putting the odontological slip down to a typing error and assuring me that the article had been considered at length by qualified readers — and as proof, she included the ten-line "expert appraisal" and two-and-a-half-page "Critical Assessment", in tiny handwriting.

The "Appraisal" approved the article for publication on condition that its latter part be dropped,[1] but recommended that a second reviewer be asked to corroborate. The "Critical Assessment" contained the considerations of this second reader, adamantly against publication.

In the following pages I shall address the consultant's criticisms point-by-point and in order. First of all, let it be noted that in this "report" I found:

- 3 serious counts of historical inaccuracy
- 5 errors deriving from a lack of familiarity with Aristotle's works
- 8 crucial errors of interpretation of Aristotle's writings
- 3 paralogisms (fallacious arguments)

- 2 reversals of my text's intended meaning
- 3 spelling errors
- 2 other problems

That's a total of **26** errors/blunders/flaws in all, or **10** per page on average.

Considering the position of said expert as a consultant to a major Brazilian academic journal, the above is reason enough to bury one's face in one's hands and wonder aloud: What in the Lord's name is happening to this country?

I. On the Bibliography

1. The consultant begins by flagging the author's failure to remain abreast of bibliographical developments:

> The author appears not to be familiar with the vast bibliography on Aristotle published in recent years, either in specialist journals, congressional annals, theses or books, and which greatly surpasses his narrow frame of scholastic interpretation and "stereotypical image which time has sedimented as acquired truth". The fact that the countering of an Aristotle "guardian of schizophrenia" (the scholastic Aristotle) with an Aristotle framed as "Apostle of Unity" is presented as a "shocking" discovery would seem to indicate that the author has not accompanied the debate in course at various centers of research...

The critiqued article contests the interpretations of Aristotle that see a separation or radical opposition between the poetic-rhetorical and dialectical-analytical discourses in the Stagirite's thought.

Is that the kind of interpretation long surpassed by the "vast bibliography" in studies on the theme? Is contesting it the academic equivalent of kicking a dead cat? The consultant assures me that it is; that only an uninformed novice would present such a contestation as a "shocking discovery".

However, it is surprising that the expert asserts some lines later that the discourses of the poets and the jurists belong to another register that does not lead to scientific discourse, *but away from it*. The discourses of poets and rhetoricians neither introduce nor prepare the ground for the discourse of science, because *the latter actually constitutes a rupture from them*...

It's baffling. On one hand, the reader says that the dualist vision of Aristotelian theory of discourse is a museum piece no longer worth contesting, yet, on the other, proceeds to defend precisely that as their own personal opinion.

The reader accuses me of kicking a dead cat at the same time as he parades the cat in the full flourish of life. And the poor creature, dragged onto the stage like this, is meowing nonstop.

Either the consultant does not know enough about the present state of the debate to see that the old opinion remains very much alive, or does not know their own position sufficiently well to understand that they actually subscribe to it.

My hypothesis is that both are true: there is no true grasp of either the former or the latter. Assessing my knowledge and self-knowledge through the lens of the reader's own, they figured they could bluff their way through.

2. A bluff indeed, because, in decrying my lack of familiarity with the recent bibliography on the matter, they fail to mention a single pertinent work I have overlooked and which might have led me to reformulate my argument and conclusions.[2] And how would they, after all, seeing as the theme has been barely touched upon by scholars? As I state clearly in the article, my theme is a stubborn absence in the bibliography and has been since St. Thomas Aquinas.

A call for an extensive bibliography on a theme where none exists could only come from someone who is themself unfamiliar with the current state of Aristotle scholarship.

3. It is true that, on many points, the scholastic interpretations of Aristotle are old hat. On many points, but not those I address. As anyone up to spec on the bibliography will know, the point I raise has not even been discussed. Isolated aspects of the theory of discourses have been broached, yes, and with a certain frequency, but serve little to confirm or refute my interpretation of the whole set. It is precisely the prevailing silence about this theme that makes it possible for the dualistic interpretation of Aristotle's theory of the discourses to penetrate so deeply into the mental habits of Western intellectuals, to the point that it has become an unconscious presupposition. An unconscious presupposition is an idea in which people believe without actually realizing it. It dominates and manipulates them from the shadows without any importance ever being placed on it. Thin-skinned enough on this issue to be scratched by a dead cat, the consultant self-proves to be the very personification of this.

II. Originality démodé

The consultant goes on:

> The author presents a thesis he considers revolutionary and innovative... which, without shadow of doubt, is totally original, but which...etc. etc.

Flattering, but, once again, baffling. How can a thesis be original if, through its author's ignorance of the current bibliography, it does nothing but rehash old, outmoded theses?

III. Too many subjects for just one book

Next, the consultant enumerates some "serious errors" they claim to have found in my work:

> Aristotle did not only address the discourses in the works catalogued as the Organon; both the Poetics and the Rhetoric, as well as Book IV of the Metaphysics, analyze discourse—the discourse of the sophists, the poets, the jurists and the scientists.

Wrong. Book IV of the *Metaphysics*—more correctly, Book Gamma of the *Metaphysics*, as the Roman numbering is only adopted in less academic editions (I would hope the consultant's knowledge of Aristotle is not limited to these)—does not deal with an analysis of discourse, but with the concept of "first philosophy". Not even a genius like Aristotle would have been able to prescribe the limits and terrain of a new science in a little over a dozen pages and still find the time to discuss *the discourse of the sophists, the poets, the jurists and so forth...*

IV. The introductory sciences

While recognizing that Aristotle discussed discourse in works other than those contained in the Organon, the consultant affirms:

> This does not justify the inclusion of the Rhetoric and Poetics among the "introductory sciences", as these are considered introductory in relation to the "first science" or "sought science" later called metaphysics.

Utterly wrong. The dialectic and logic—sciences in the *Organon*—are not introductory only to metaphysics, but to *the theoretical sciences in general and even to the practical/technical sciences*. And it could not be otherwise, because, for Aristotle, the sciences form a system and the *Organon* is an introduction to that system, not this or that science in particular. This is so obvious that not even a novice could fail to see it. Only lines later, the consultant, with that unique coherency that characterizes their reasoning, recognizes that dialectic is the method of Ethics.

V. Apophantic

Further on:

107

> The discourse of poets and the discourse of jurists belong to another
> register and do not lead to the discourse of science, rather they move
> away from it, as "other discourses". This distinction is made clear when
> Aristotle restricts his analyses to "logos apophantikos", the only one to
> encompass the question of truth/falsity, and distinguishes it from interjec-
> tion and supplication (expressions of feeling and desire). The "apophan-
> tic" function of scientific discourse, a notion absolutely central to
> Aristotle, is totally ignored by the author.

Dearie me! Never would I have thought I'd live to see a philosophy lecturer confuse *apophantic* and *apodeictic*!

Apophantic, dear consultant, is simply a declarative statement which either asserts or denies something, whilst an interjection or supplication affirms or denies nothing whatsoever. How can anyone suppose that the discourse of science (logico-analytical discourse) alone is apophantic and that the other discourses make no assertions or denials? When a lawyer claims his client is innocent, is he not making an assertion? And when the judge issues a guilty verdict all the same, is she not denying that assertion and affirming something else? When the epic tells us that Telemachus left in search of his father but found nothing, are we to understand it makes no affirmations? Certainly, nothing so ridiculous ever passed through Aristotle's head.

The *four* discourses are apophantic, and equally so: they all affirm and deny something; their statements can —each in its own way and to its own degree—be true or false. None of the four discourses is mere interjection or appeal.

They do, however, differ in the level of truth they can

aspire to, or rather the level of credibility they can claim. Scientific discourse stands over and above as the only demonstrative discourse, capable of irrefutable proof. In other words, it's the only one that is apodeictic—that's *apodeictic*, zounds! Not *apophantic*.

The consultant's confusion on this is so bush-league, so basic, that I'm left with a mix of disgust and pity to have to spell it out to an academic, a consultant for one of the largest academic institutions in the country. It is, frankly, distressing.

I do not wish to belabor the point, but, just by way of example, I need to ask our consultant how they can reconcile the notion of poetry as *mimesis* (something which they claim I ignore) with the assertion that scientific discourse alone is apophantic? How can the poet imitate reality without making affirmations or refutations about it?

What's more, Aristotle declares that poetry "is more philosophical than History", as it speaks of man in general, while History deals only with the particular. How could poetry speak general truths about humankind without making assertions or denials and limiting itself to moans and interjections?

It is true that Aristotle excluded the study of non-apophantic statements from the analytical, attributing them to poetics and rhetoric. By that I mean statements that limit themselves to expressing desires, requests or orders.[3] But it would be abusive to say the least to contend, on the strength of that, that the philosopher wished to limit poetics and rhetoric to that type of sentence alone, excluding from their remit all apophantic statements. Any such intent on Aristotle's part would simply render both unviable as sciences, emptying the concepts of possibility and verisimilitude of all meaning. To say "analytical logic only deals with apophantic propositions" is not the same as saying "only analytical logic deals with apophantic propositions". What Aristotle wanted to say is, clearly, that the study of poetics and rhetoric also deals with sentence types that lie beyond the strict interests of the analytical sciences—something that ought to be pretty obvious.

VI. The function of dialectic

As for his considerations on Dialectic, the author ignores the function which Aristotle (begrudgingly) attributes to it when it comes to establishing the principles of the analytical.

1. When I say that the four sciences of discourse are inseparable, that they form an ascending scale of credibility that corresponds to the degrees which man ascends from sensory perceptions to apodeictic rational knowledge, it should be obvious that each discourse lays the terrain for the next. How, I ask, could I have said that—as I do—whilst ignoring, or never knowing, the function dialectic fulfills in the pursuit of analytical principles? That's something that truly beggars human understanding.

2. When they insert the word "begrudgingly" in brackets, the consultant demonstrates their own appreciation for the old image of Aristotle which he himself dismisses as outmoded and surpassed, because it means Aristotle recognized the debt analytical logic owed to dialectic. And

why "begrudgingly"? Implicit in the expression is a certain disdain Aristotle supposedly felt for dialectic, when, in fact, the growing trend in Aristotelian exegesis (on which the consultant claims to be so up to speed) is to recognize the validity of Weil's thesis, according to which dialectic is, for Aristotle, the method *par excellence*, and to which the analytical is but an extension and complement.[4] Evidently, I subscribe wholeheartedly to that thesis. And that is why I see in this parenthetical inclusion a sign that the consultant remains partial to that old image of Aristotle which they contest in my work: an image under which dialectic is shorn of all but a specific and secondary function.

And from that I derive priceless counsel: before dismissing a dead cat, always make sure it's not a living lion.

VII. Save me, St. Gregory!

Next, the all-knowing decides to give me some lessons in History:

"The Western Aristotelianism that developed over that vast period from the eve of the Christian Era all the way to the Renaissance". The author's affirmation is entirely false, seeing as, 'at the eve of the Christian Era', Aristotle was unknown to the Church fathers and would only become so in Europe during the Late Middle Ages (12th Century), thanks to invading Arabs, to the Toledo School of Translators, and, later, to Saints Gregory the Great and Thomas Aquinas.

To these lessons, all I can say is:

1. Saint Gregory the Great can't have done anything at all in the 12th Century, much less later, as he died in the year 604. The Saint writing about Aristotle at the time was *Albert* the Great (darn typos again!).

But, even with respect to St. Albert it would be absurd to claim that he was a disseminator of Aristotle's thought in Christian Europe, as he only wrote his *Commentaries* to calm all the fuss over the Stagirite's *Physics,* which, by defending the hypothesis of the world's eternity, seemed to butt heads rather directly with the Scripture. Now, as a work nobody knew could cause no furor, evidently Albert's own writings were not penned to *introduce* Aristotle to the Continent but were an effect rather than a cause of their dissemination. Thomas, for his part, came after Albert, his mentor, and whose *Commentaries* he actually completed.

2. The idea that Aristotle was only known in the West after the 12th Century may prevail in paperback guides, but there is not a single specialist in the field who does not know it's untrue. What the Arabs brought to the West were Aristotle's books on *Physics.* The logics and *Metaphysics,* at the very least, were being read—in versions of varying quality, plain or with commentary, loved or hated —in Christian Europe since the first centuries AD. They are quoted and discussed, with different degrees of precision and at varying lengths in countless passages from Saint Augustine, in Clement of Alexandria (2nd Century), Eusebius of Caesarea (3rd Century), Saint Isidore of Seville (6th Century), by the anonymous author of *Confutatio dogmatum quorundam Aristotelicorium* (400 AD), Irenaeus of Lyon (2nd Century), Marius Victorinus (3rd Century),

Arnobius of Sicca (3ʳᵈ Century), Firmicius Maternus (4ᵗʰ Century), Marcellus of Ancyra (4ᵗʰ Century), Saint Basil the Great (4ᵗʰ Century), Eunomius of Cyzicus (3ʳᵈ Century), Nemesius of Emesa (4ᵗʰ Century), and Theodoret of Cyrus (5ᵗʰ Century). And let's not forget that, already in Patristic times, there was a whole Christian theological school inspired by Aristotle (the Antioch School), and that Boethius's translations of Aristotle himself and of the Commentaries of Porphyry existed long before the translators of Toledo had even been born or Albert and Thomas had yet wriggled spermatozoon tails.[5]

And that's just what I—a complete ignoramus in all things pertaining to Aristotelian bibliography—was able to locate. I imagine the consultant, an individual far better informed than I, could find so much more if they deigned to study the subject before trying to teach it.

Well, one might ask, if I had consulted all these authors, why did I not cite them? Simple: because, of everything they said about Aristotle, I found nothing of direct relevance to my project, and the purpose of citations is to be pertinent, not parade erudition willy-nilly, as the consultant would have me do.

3. Anyone who is not familiar with the classic sources on a theme and knows the subject only from more recent contributions to the bibliography cannot be considered an expert, merely a diligent novice at best. Here I'm supposing that my consultant actually knows the recent bibliography and yet I fear not, for a reading of the works of Dumont, Düring, Millet, Barnes, or, going further back, of Brentano, Jaeger, Ravaisson, Hamelin, Mansion, Le Blond, Ross and *tutti quanti* would certainly have revealed the impossibility of opining on the subject based on them alone, and without recourse to the primary sources. If my consultant had actually read the primary sources, they would hardly have said the things they did.

VIII. Not a single shot on target

"Above all, dialectic was a Platonic relic, absorbed into and surpassed by analytical logic." While Aristotle considers the analytical a more rigorous method proper to science than Platonic dialectic, that does not mean to say he considered dialectic "absorbed and surpassed"...

1. Finally the consultant says something we can agree on: indeed, Aristotle, having built his logic, preserves dialectic as a valid method. The consultant rightly opposes the belief that "dialectic was a Platonic relic, absorbed and surpassed in analytical logic". However, for some strange reason they attribute the offending opinion to me, without noticing that it was precisely the notion I was vehemently rejecting.

In fact, it is the opinion held by the Solmsen school, against which, endorsing Weil, I was arguing on that precise occasion.[6] I did not cite Solmsen by name in the article, but there was no need to do so, as the position he upheld was that being taken apart in the passage I quoted from Eric Weil.

What was the consultant's purpose in attributing to me an opinion I contest? Was it to more readily refute it, presenting someone else's argument as their own? Or was it simply because they don't know how to read?

IX. Dialectic, again

Having rescued dialectic in Aristotle's name, the consultant pulls out all the stops and claims that it only remains a valid method because

> There are fields of knowledge and being which, not being governed by necessity, cannot be approached analytically.

1. Perhaps the consultant would be good enough to explain to me how a dialectic restricted to fields "not governed by necessity" might establish, as they contended earlier, the principles of analytical logic? Are those principles, then, merely probabilistic and "not governed by necessity"?

2. In fact, Aristotle attributed a much more decisive role to dialectic than that of an *ad hoc* logic for fields "not governed by necessity". His writings are very clear on this point, and assign to dialectic a triple function: first, it is a logic of the probable, or the reasonable; second, it is a pedagogical practice that trains the spirit for scientific discussion; and third, it is a method for finding the founding principles of any new science.[7]

3. In short, the dialectic which Aristotle retains is not Platonic, but his own, and very different to Plato's in function, technique and finality.

X. On disinterested knowledge

> "The four sciences of discourse deal with the four ways in which one can, through words, influence others' minds." With this statement the author

once again ignores the concept of apophantic logic and the assertion that theoretical science is "disinterested and non-utilitarian"—a condition of its objectivity and freedom. Theoretical science does not aim to "influence others' minds", but to manifest being through discourse.

1. The consultant reoffends in confusing the terms apophantic and apodeictic, and I have said all I plan to say on that matter.

2. When Aristotle says that theoretical knowledge is disinterested, what he means is that it does not pursue any *practical* ends. He certainly does not mean to say that true knowledge is not a desirable end in and of itself, much less that the demonstration of truth, enacted in logico-analytical discourse, has no influence over the listener. On the contrary, apodeictic demonstration exercises the most unimpeachable influence insofar as it offers conclusions that must be accepted by all capable of understanding them. As Clement of Alexandria (one of the priests the consultant insists had never heard of Aristotle) said on the matter, "logical fact derived from demonstrations produces, in the soul of those who have followed the demonstrative chain, a faith so powerful that it cannot even imagine the demonstrated fact being different to the way it is, rendering null all force of doubt that might insinuate itself upon the spirit in order to deceive it".[8]

The distinction between the dialectic and analytical cannot be clearly conceived other than through a concrete *situation of discourse*, the difference in the relation between speaker and listener: "The difference [between dialectic and analytical discourse]", says Eric Weil, is, for Aristotle, "the same as that between the course given by a teacher and a group discussion, or, otherwise put, between a scientific monologue and a dialogue."[9]

When the master manifests—apophantically—the truth of being in his monologue, do the rigor and the objectivity of science really entail that the listener should remain mute and indifferent?

Our consultant sets up a false opposition between "influencing others' minds" and "demonstrating the truth" and attributes it to Aristotle himself, who would never have accepted such a thing.

XI. Poetics and mimesis

Tireless in their pursuit of my blunders, the consultant continues:

> The Poetics is not about the possible (that, according to Aristotle, is the subject of the Rhetoric), but about a literary genre, Tragedy... The author completely ignores the central role of *mimesis* and *catharsis*.

1. The *Poetics* is not about tragedy, but about poetry *in general*, of which tragedy is but one modality. It is true that all that remains of the original treatise are the introduction and the section on tragedy, but the disappearance of the rest was certainly not in Aristotle's plans, and the introduction contains sufficient clues as to what he had to say about poetics in general.

2. As for the consultant's contention that the *Poetics* is not about the possible, Aristotle himself, having classified the literary work as a sort of *mimesis* or imitation, clarifies

"that it is not the function of the poet to relate what has happened, but what may happen, what is possible according to the law of probability or necessity."[10]

Only a very distracted reader could fail to recognize right there the two elements that, in Aristotle's method, comprise a definition: collection into genus and division into species. Poetry is collected under the genus *mimesis*, insofar as it is an imitation of life, yet its specific difference is that it does not imitate actual life (history), but possible life.

The imitation of the possible is the very definition of the poetic work, and anyone who fails to bear that definition in mind will understand very little of what Aristotle goes on to say about tragedy. That is precisely the case with our consultant—according to whom, however, it is I who am oblivious to the central role of *mimesis*. Which role—sweet patience!—if not that expressed in Aristotle's own definition?

As for *catharsis*, about which the consultant would have us believe I know absolutely nothing, I do know this: that, for Aristotle, *catharsis* could not occur if poetry, like history, were to imitate the real rather than the possible, because, as Aristotle insists, the real is always particular, while the possible is generic. It is precisely because it imitates the generic and not the particular that "poetry is more philosophical and a higher thing than history".[11] Now, "the particular [or historically real] is—for example —what Alcibiades did or suffered" and is of more interest to Alcibiades than to anyone else. The generic, on the other hand, interests all men: if we are moved by the hero's downfall, it is not because it is the misfortune of A or B, but the possible fate of us all. If poetry were to imitate the historical reality as such, there could be no *catharsis*, due to the unbridgeable—and almost Brechtian —alienation effect captured in Shakespeare's famous question: "What's Hecuba to him, or he to Hecuba?".[12] The definition of poetry as imitation of the possible leads us to the heart of the mystery of *catharsis*—another Greek word which the consultant uses only as part of the bluff of erudition, being incapable of grasping the clearest implications of the concept.[13]

XII. *Verossímel?*

Still on the same subject:

According to Aristotle, the verisimilar [misspelled here in Portuguese] is a key element of tragedy—so it is hard to see how it could come to be a defining characteristic of rhetoric.

1. First of all, friend, *verossímel* my eye [the correct spelling is *verossímil*]! And don't come with that old excuse that it's a typo, because you write this abomination no fewer than three times.

2. As for the *verossímil*, the probable, there is an obvious difference between poetic verisimilitude and rhetorical verisimilitude. In his definition of poetry, Aristotle uses the expression "possible probability", insofar as what counts in rhetorical argumentation is the probable as possible, or, otherwise put, the "probably real". There's no confusion here: rhetorical argument has to be true-to-life in the sense that it imitates the real, the historical, and

not merely the possible. A prosecutor, for example, does not endeavor to demonstrate the possibility of a defendant's guilt (asking the jury to 'suspend disbelief' concerning culpability), but his actual guilt. The defense attorney, on the other hand, only needs to seed the possibility of innocence, without having to demonstrate actual innocence based on incontrovertible proof. The verisimilitude, here, consists in rhetorical persuasion, a strong fixing of the will, though without dialectically conclusive proof, much less apodeictic demonstration. In the poetic work, on the other hand, the viewer/reader need only entertain the *possibility* of the events—and, in this sense, the demand for verisimilitude is loosened, according to the Aristotelian rule that the "likely can sometimes transpire in unlikely ways". If, on the other hand, the viewer/reader accepts the events as real, getting his narrative wires crossed and mistaking poetry for rhetoric, the poetry is immediately drained of its cathartic effect, because it would now be speaking solely of "Alcibiades", not all humanity. To be persuaded of a possibility is not the same thing as being persuaded of a fact.

The confusion is silly to say the least.

3. Aristotle himself employs the term "probable" to define the type of credibility proper to rhetoric. The consultant's qualms about it reveal nothing but lack of knowledge of the Greek text, in which the word πιθανός leaves no room for the slightest doubt on this point.

It is a scandal that an academic work can be submitted for assessment to someone who only knows the subject second hand and cannot even adequately evaluate the use of vocabulary.

XIII. Tragedy and metaphysics

"On the unlimited opening of the world of possibilities"...the author's affirmation is incorrect. There is no "unlimited opening" in the world of possibilities in Aristotle, as act precedes potency, the possible is entirely determined by the potentialities contained in the real.

1. My dear consultant, have you read what you wrote? It's pure nonsense. If act precedes potency, how can it be determined by it? Ah, I know: it must have been another typo!

2. Even reshaped into something a little more logically coherent, the reasoning remains false, as, for Aristotle, the potency of the first (uncaused) cause is infinite.[14] This "positive" infinitude of the first cause cannot replicate itself as infinite in the effects it produces, and the result is that, on the cosmic scale, the infinitude that was supreme perfection in the divine becomes defect, incompleteness, privation, accident in creation, because "nature flees from the infinite [...] and always seeks an end".[15] Of course, the potency contained in any singular being only predetermines the possibilities of its *normal* development, but has no control over the accidents that befall it along the way. Accidents are, in principle, unlimited and unlimitable: as inverted reflections of divine infinitude, they do not derive from the potency of the being that suffers them, but from divine potency itself. Their root does not lie in the "positive" constitution of the finite being, but in its incommensurability with the infinite. Hence any being, with its own limited, determined potency, is, at the same time, subject to unlimited accidents. The incommensurability between

the divine and the cosmic is such that, on the cosmic scale, *the accidental exists as a matter of necessity*, and it is from this surprising and almost paradoxical connection between necessity and accident that the fundamental inspiration for one of the main literary genres is born: tragedy. In tragedy the accidents—not the normal developments as per the realization of potency in act—link into a shackle-chain of fate, in accordance with a sort of logic of the absurd, which only Grace (one notion of ours which is absent in Greek philosophy) can break. If possibilities were predetermined by the potency of finite beings alone, as the consultant seems to think they are, *tragedy would be absolutely impossible, for everything would unfurl according to the blueprint latent in each and every finite being and there would be no accidents, much less the metaphysically necessary accident that constitutes the core of tragic conflict.* Tragedy opens to the unlimited inputs of the possible, because if it did not, there could be no tragedy at all.

Yes, my friend: it's great using words like catharsis, mimesis, apophantic, act and potency, etc. to impress the layman and come across as intellectual and wise. But words are spiteful, and conceal their meanings from those who would disrespect them by using them for the purposes of showing off.

XIV. Historical evolution

One cannot speak of historical evolution in Aristotle. As a Greek, Aristotle's concept of time is circular, non-linear; time eternally returns upon itself, so there is no way one can speak of History at the core of Aristotelian thought.

1. What sort of nonsense is this? Even the founder of historicism, Giambattista Vico himself, had a circular conception of time—his famous *corsi e ricorsi* (courses and recourses). So does that mean we cannot speak of History at the core of Vico's thought either?

2. As everyone except our consultant will know, Aristotle was the first to introduce an historical lens in his approach to philosophical questions, not to mention the very first attempts at genetic explanation in the natural sciences and gnoseology. That's sufficient to make him, amongst Greeks at least, the precursor of modern historicism and evolutionism. It's obvious that we're dealing here with historicism in embryonic form, but who said it was anything more than that?

3. Not once does Aristotle affirm the circularity of time. What he does posit is the First Cause.[16] And if he defines time as "the measure of movement" (a measure tracked by the soul),[17] and says that the act of the First Cause is infinite, it should be abundantly clear that there is no temporal measurement in the "circularity" of the movement of the First Cause, which has nothing whatsoever to do with the circularity of time. To suggest that Aristotle, as a Greek, had to think like other Greeks is pure silliness: a philosopher's thought cannot be deduced from the commonly held beliefs of their time, but only from reading their works.[18] To assume that any given member of a community must be mentally limited to the *doxa* of the time is to condemn society to never producing a single philosopher. It's an idea that dispenses with the need to wrangle with what is written, as the gist would already be served up in a handful of atrociously primary sociological generalizations. Unfortunately, it's a vice for which there would seem to be no cure in Brazil.

XV. And still not a shot on target

Failing yet again to understand what I say, the consultant prefers to attribute to me what I did not say— preferably some patent absurdity that can be readily debunked in the pretense of demolishing my arguments by batting away some hogwash of their own invention. In this, the consultant is a repeat offender, but in the following case outdoes themselves for sheer shamelessness:

> To locate Dialectic in the Patristic Era is to ignore reality...etc. etc.

Yes, of course it is. And it would have been absurd of me to do such a thing. But I did precisely the opposite. What is actually said in my work is: "Dialectical discourse [...] did not become socially dominant [...] until the end of the Patristic Period."[19] Why is it that, whenever the consultant agrees with me, he feels the need to impute to me the opposite opinion? Is it that hard for him to admit that I was, in fact, right about something?

XVI. The Four Discourses in Time

Next up, the hapless consultant proffers a general law of their own concerning the development of cultures, which is intended to contest mine:

I. De re Aristotelica Opiniones Abominandae: The Dead Cat's...

...in many cultures, the so-called four discourses co-exist and are applied to different spheres of human reality and political life. To attempt to establish the "primacy" of any one discourse seems to us an anachronous resurrection of positivist discourse and its Law of Three Stages.[20]

I. Now there is a revolutionary development: each culture develops the four forms of discourse simultaneously, and none predominates. Fantastic! In other words, the science of rhetoric did *not* develop in Greece before Socratic dialectic; that Tertullian and Origen's apologetic rhetoric did *not* precede the dialectic of the Christian doctrine devised by the scholastics; that Islamic rhetoric did *not* reach its height in Imam 'Ali centuries before the success of dialectic with Al-Ghazzali, Avicenna and Ibn 'Arabi; and that logico-scientific discourse actually arose in cultures throughout the world *at the same time* and found its fullest expression in mythopoetic discourse, as is clearly evidenced by the scientifically-accepted fact that the mythologies and symbolic art of the primitive cultures —from the Pygmies and Bantus to the Indians of the Upper Xingu, to name but a few—came down to us along with their treatises in logic, mathematical physics, and so forth.

That all human beings, regardless of historical moment, possess the same aptitude—potency—for the four discourses is undeniable (and, indeed, to reason it out in Aristotelian fashion, indispensable for any succession of the discourses over time), but to pretend that all four manifested historically as expressions of culture at the same time is unadulterated nonsense.

On the other hand, we also know that mythopoetic

discourse can be gravid with knowledge of scientific value, as has so often been the case. But that does not make mythopoetic discourse logico-analytical *in form*. And it should be abundantly clear to anyone who can read that my work here is about the succession of forms of discourse, not their content.

2. As for the mention of the Law of the Three Stages, it's a simple association of ideas, and too vague to be anything more than impertinent. More plausible would have been the association with the Marxist theory of the succession *primitive community/ feudalism/ capitalism/ socialism*, which at least coincides with my theory in number of stages. However, if the consultant is wont to judge scientific theories by the associations of ideas they might fortuitously suggest, then their true vocation is for the occult, not science.

XV. Conclusion

Both the consultant in the "Critical Appraisal" and the editor in the brief "Technical report" that precedes it took issue, above all, with the idea of a historical succession of the discourses, which is described as "extremely naive" by the former, and "based on very fragile foundations" by the latter.

Of course, the idea is presented at the end of my work without any pretension toward serving as exhaustive proof, but merely as an example of the live potentialities of Aristotelian thought and its capacity to confront us, even now, with relevant intellectual challenges. The succession model which Aristotle's writings suggest, and which the facts support as highly plausible, is one such challenge, and it was precisely in this spirit that it was presented. Rather than take the work as an opportunity to engage in serious discussion, these parties preferred to take offense and reject the ideas presented under a hail of futile allegations. The critical evaluator made neither critique nor evaluation, merely trotted out figures of speech. The author of the "technical report", for their part, seems to have felt a single adjective—"naive"—was enough to put an end to the matter. Not only does this individual have an overblown notion of their own importance, but seems to think that improvised opinion can be passed off as expertise with a little condescension.

As for the consultant, this critical appraisal has merely landed them, as I have shown, in a bit of a bind. Mediocre mentalities, accustomed as they are to identifying scientific rigor with attention to finer points (important, yet not always sufficient in itself), tend to dismiss as mere pretension any wider theoretical explanation that does not come with the soothing endorsement of whatever celebrity thinker happens to be in vogue. They therefore balk at examining these explanations and inadvertently revert to *principium auctoritatis*, corroding the scientific spirit they purport to defend.

People who go about their business in this manner should think twice before calling anyone else naive. To be naive means to presuppose, without any solid grounds or well-founded arguments, that events proceeded in the History of this or that culture in accordance with an order of succession other than the one presented in my Aristotelian model. Because any inversion of that order would be highly unlikely at best, as should become clear to anyone who bothered to ask themselves the following questions:

1. Can a culture develop an art of political discussion before first having a mythopoetic repertoire on which the community's feelings and values rest and upon which the public credibility of its arguments must depend?

2. Is it possible to develop a dialectic—art of rational triage—without there first being arguments in dispute?

3. Can a culture develop a technique of apodeictic demonstration before first having a practice and art of discussion?

What's more, only in the most superficial appearance of its schema could the idea of succession remind anyone of the old and peremptory generalizations of Comte, Marx, Brunschvicq, Sorokin and the like. It is not, first and foremost, a causal hypothesis, but the simple descriptive schema of a fact to which the chronology of events attests: mythopoetic discourse arose first, rhetoric came second, then dialectic and, following upon that, analytical discourse. Aristotle himself, in formulating dialectic and laying the groundwork for the analytical, was very much aware that it was the culmination of all Greek thought that had gone before; and, if he did not extend that model to the description of other cultures, that does not mean that we cannot do so in his name, albeit with a two-point-four-millennia delay. In fact, *to do so is mandatory, seeing as an elementary precept of the scientific method obliges us to test the primary hypotheses before moving on to the secondary.*

Secondly, the succession does not imply any notion of "progress" in the qualitative sense, much less any global teleology of History, as do the theories of Comte and Marx. To dismiss it summarily as naive, wave it away as some throwback to the metaphysical dead-ends of History, is a rhetorical approach that is simply unbecoming of true scientists. One doesn't judge a theory by its vague and surface similarities to other theories.

The author of the Report—admittedly more restrained and sensible than the consultant—obviously did not ask themselves the three questions above, and does not appear capable of citing *a single example* of a culture in which the chronological succession of events diverged from the presented model. They reject the hypothesis on the grounds of mere irrational antipathy, believing—disingenuously or maliciously—that an adjective is as good as a refutation. Most surprising of all is the total lack of curiosity, an arrogant laziness that, between one yawn and another, simply dismisses a question so as not to have to give it any thought, and goes back to sleep without entertaining the possibility that they might be missing something. It is this false sense of superiority that transforms the Third-world intellectual into a specific "type": this sublime indifference that, like Antonio Machado's "Wretched Castile, once noble/ and wrapped in rags, scorns what it does not know".[21]

I do, however, commend the decision to escalate the matter for a second opinion.

As for the author of the "Critical Appraisal", I have demonstrated in the preceding pages just how little he knows of the subject. He is a veritable bluff artist, fluent in Javanese,[22] whose presence on the Editorial Committee of a serious journal like *Ciência Hoje* is—to put it mildly—a tropical extravagance. I hope against hope that it's a young man, with time ahead of him to quit posturing and embark on an authentic academic career, for which he undoubtedly has the talent, but lacks the scruples without which all talent becomes fertile ground for error and damage. Should he feel humiliated upon reading these words, lucky him: shame, said Nietzsche, is the mother of all learning. Needless to say, I put myself at his disposal for any supplementary explanations he may require, and it would be a pleasure to engage with him without any ill feelings whatsoever, confident that, should he heed the Biblical warning that a rebuke ought never be disdained, there is still a chance he might become someone.

Please note that at no time did I question the journal's right to decline publication, and its decision not to publish is no grand matter. In October, having not heard back from the SBPC, I went ahead and published the work in book form—rendering any future reply from *Ciência Hoje* perfectly moot.

When I wrote to the journal on October 24, it was not in the spirit of contesting the decision—which would have been uselessly late and childishly insolent— but merely to express my bafflement as to the frankly comical reasons for it.

However, upon receiving the reply from Dr. Yonne and reading the attached documents, I was left altogether stupefied, scandalized and, to tell the truth, more than a little incensed. Not because I felt, personally, the victim of an injustice—an inferior sentiment much abused in our day—but because I was once again seeing one of the most noble intellectual pursuits of all usurped by the proclivity toward pseudo-intellectualism that is, along with the ethical bankruptcy of our politicians, one of our nation's worst scourges. The ethics of intellectual life is a prerequisite for a nation's moral regeneration, and in Brazil, time and again, we see intellectuals eager to sit as judges of public morality before first going about their duties with anything resembling ethical probity. For me, having a man who "speaks Javanese" infiltrated into our universities and cultural institutions is every bit as scandalous and prejudicial to the nation as any João Alves or P.C. Farias.[23] Worse than either, I would say, because while they chip away at public funds, bluffers like the consultant corrupt the soul and intelligence, the supreme patrimony upon which rests the dignity of the human being.

Rio de Janeiro, November 9, 1994

II. Challenge to the Usurpers behind Closed Ranks

The waspish readiness to opine on a text they haven't read is clear indication of the mentality of Carlos Henrique Escobar and Gilberto Velho.[1] The former, taking umbrage with some things I said about his comrades in ideology[2] which were expressed in an article that has nothing whatsoever to do with the case at hand, felt himself entitled to venture some frankly scattershot judgements on a matter he knows nothing about—an action unbefitting of a man of science, but typical of the ideologue and cheap propagandist, incapable of seeing issues unless through the lens of his political persuasions. As for Gilberto Velho, he resorts to the facile strategy of putting words in my mouth: at no time did I complain of "discrimination". How could a consultant I do not know discriminate against an author he has never heard of? What I did complain about is having been subjected to an incompetent evaluator. Professor Ênio Candotti also manages to skirt the issue by wondering out loud what "would happen" if every dissatisfied submitter to an academic journal were to question the decision in such terms. What would happen is that the SBPC's consultant panel would feature neither the inept fellow who assessed my article nor "stars" presumptuous enough to hold forth on papers they haven't even read. The Brazilian academic establishment wants to play judge and jury on the whole nation but can't bear to be second-guessed itself. On folks like these Karl Kraus once said: "they judge so as to avert judgment". Prof. Candotti says there is no reason for all the fuss. *Yet he, through omission, was solely responsible for the fuss.* He received a copy of my book some weeks ago, yet did nothing. And, as a result, what could have been resolved discreetly ended up in the press. All it would have taken was for Prof. Candotti to do his job and look into the matter. As Dr. Claudio Ribeiro so well said: "it's the editor's responsibility to identify such errors". That's what Prof. Candotti is there for, not to simply bat away complaints, whether through some misplaced belief in the infallibility of academia or because addressing potential problems wouldn't be worth the trouble. In fact, Prof. Candotti seems to forget that the SBPC receives public funding, *so if an irregularity is flagged, he has a duty to investigate it,* not react like an offended damsel and refuse to discuss the matter. I was very respectful to the SBPC in my letter, saying that the ineptitude of one of its members in no way reflected upon the institution's honor *in toto*. And yet Prof. Candotti, through pride and stubbornness, opted to imperil the image of the SBPC merely to avoid admitting to the shoddy work of a single member. What solidarity! Either the consultant in question is someone very important, or Prof. Candotti thinks it normal for an academic society to act like a secret society, closing ranks behind a pact of loyalty unto death.

As for Callado, his imbecilic question—"How does he manage to get into the main newspapers?"—begs a twofold answer: first, I have been a professional journalist for the last thirty years; and, second, the newspapers don't select their collaborators according to Antônio Callado's criteria. Thank the lord, Callado is not the consultant or head of personnel at a newspaper. If he were, he would certainly use his clout to veto the hiring of those not in his favor. His hypocrisy reveals itself clearly when, denying anything resembling censorship has occurred, he once again calls for newsrooms to close their doors to me. How depressing! But that's not the end of it: in calling me "unknown", Callado is either lying or going gaga, because he has known me personally for years—it was out of charity to an elderly man that I have not brought this up until now. But, beyond that, what sense does it make calling the author of books that have, as Callado knows perfectly well, been described as "stupendous" (Herberto Sales), "exceedingly important" (Bruno Tolentino), "excellent" (Josué Montello), and "magnificent" (Jacob Klintowitz), unknown?

In short, the arguments used against me in this polemic amount to nothing but a carnivalesque parade of prestige, *argumentum auctoritatis* (appeal to authority) and *argumentum baculinum* (appeal to force). And so I ask: supposing they actually read my piece, which of all these gents knows Aristotle sufficiently well to judge the matter? Bruno Tolentino is quite right when he calls them usurpers. They are every bit as much the usurper as [Fernando] Collar or João Alves: they may not steal public money, but they use their positions and circle of friendships to attribute to one another an intellectual authority they do not possess. I publicly challenge these men to debate with me, based on textual, documental evidence, the objections I made to my consultant's criticisms. They will all flee, hiding behind the shield of cliquery without which each, individually, is but a defenseless boy lost in the desert of his own ignorance. Of those interviewed, only Professor Rosângela Nunes and Dr. Claudio Ribeiro declared, with exemplary humility, that they could not possibly judge what they had not read. But both admitted, in principle at least, the *possibility* of serious flaws in the consultant's report. For the others, the hypothesis was unthinkable by definition. *SBPC locuta, causa finita* (SBPC has spoken, end of story), isn't that right? Incapable of actual debate, they deal the marked cards of officialism and cronyism.

III. Letters to Ênio Candotti

Rio de Janeiro, November 16, 1994

Dear Sir,

As suggested to me by our mutual friend, Dr. Ivan da Costa Marques, please find enclosed a copy of the document I sent to the SBPC journal addressing some recent events.[1]

Dr. Ivan and myself are of the opinion that it would be useful and fair to inform you of the somewhat unpalatable episode.

I hope you will forgive my asking you to

allot the document in question some consideration, devoting time certainly better used on other matters. I thank you in advance.

My very best regards.

Cordially,
Olavo Carvalho

∾

LETTER TWO

Rio de Janeiro, January 2, 1995

Dear Sir,

In light of your declarations to the *O Globo* newspaper on December 28, the letter which you published in the same paper the following day is a masterpiece of sheer nonsense. Alleging that the complexity of the subject might confuse the lay reader, you ask that the debate surrounding my work on Aristotle be taken out of the mainstream press and returned to the discreet pages of "a specialist publication". Am I to understand that the SBPC is recommending that a work it considered unworthy of discussion in a specialist publication should now be debated in one? Should journals specializing in philosophy be any less demanding in their selection than *Ciência Hoje*? Let's be clear on one thing: it was not out of excessive specialization that my article was rejected. Dr. Yonne was quite explicit: my paper "did not meet the minimal acceptable conditions for a scientific work". Does *Ciência Hoje* hold itself in such high esteem that it deigns to send specialist journals its rejects.

When a sensible person says insensate things, we would do well to suppose that it was either a case of momentary distraction, or ulterior motives. As distractedness would be unthinkable in such a decisive moment, I can only assume you were attempting to quash the scandal, and so, in your hurry, availed of an improvised pretext. The falsity of your position even stoops to the pseudo-literary image—of dreadfully poor taste, by the way—with which you close your letter: what you wished to conceal was not Aristotle's tooth decay—alas, History has left us no indication of the state of the philosopher's dental health—so much as the cancer of pseudo-intellectuality that gnaws at the innards of the SBPC.

The only serious dental problem I found in Aristotle was his famous tooth count in women, who, he claims, have more gnashers than men (*Aristotelis insignis negligentia*). On cavities and the like, he made no complaint, though we might have to refer to the famous peripatetic odontological specialist Dr Yonne Leite on that matter, for she will certainly have more luck filling those than she did the holes in the consultant's report on my work.

Your declaration to the newspaper reflects the haughtiness of a social elite that is not used to being beaten with its own whipping stick and firmly believes that it should be considered at all times above suspicion. Always accusing, denouncing, pontificating, the SBPC ended up being molded by its own pulpit, and incorporating it into itself as second nature, forgetting in the process that, as it benefits from public funds, it has to render account of itself too. Your question—what would happen if every submitter were to object to the evaluator's opinion and decide to complain—is silly, to say the least. What would happen, if indeed you do not know, is this:

1. The SBPC journal would not make such poor use of public money paying for the services of inept consultants (perhaps there aren't many of these, but how are we to know that if no come back is permitted?);

2. It would soon learn to be humble, and to respect the public, becoming self-critical and exigent towards itself, rather than sitting back on the presumption of its own infallibility, like some grand priestly caste—currently under the pontiff Ennius I.

However, if you really wanted to deal with this matter quietly among scholars, Your Holiness should have acted with more celerity upon receipt of the copy I sent you of my responses to the "critical appraisal". After all, it was sent some weeks before the case was brought to the attention of the press.[2] As you did nothing then, it makes no sense for you to complain about the scandal now, as it is the fruit of the womb of your own omission.

As for your paternal concern for the layman's soul—as if, when it comes to Aristotle, yourself and Dr. Yonne weren't laypeople too!—, it is a smoke screen and nothing more. It's not the public that has something to fear from this debacle; it's the SBPC. Among the millions of readers of *O Globo*, I am sure there are more cultured individuals better versed in the matter than the consultants on the *Ciência Hoje* editorial committee.[3] However illustrious the members of this committee may consider themselves, they are not a new Holy See invested with the authority to decide what the public is or is not mature enough to know. Pretending to protect the public, the SBPC protects only itself, concealing the ineptitude of its editorial committee under a mantle of opacity woven with the discourse of transparency.

I have never held the Brazilian intellectual milieu in high regard, much less the academic community, but, on recommendation of our mutual friend Dr. Ivan da Costa Marques, I had expected a more elegant bearing on your part.

Cordially,
Olavo de Carvalho

Appendix: Plato's Analogy of the Divided Line

(CONTRIBUTED BY: ANTHONY DOYLE)

In the *Republic* (509d–511e), Plato has Socrates draw the following analogy for Glaucon in order to illustrate the difference and relationship between the visible and intelligible realms.

Socrates asks Glaucon to imagine a line representing the entirety of human experience, and then divide that line unequally (let's say a ratio of 1:2):

Line AC represents the visible world, with AB representing the shadows and reflections of physical things, and BC, the things themselves.

But human experience goes beyond these. Imagine an extension to the line the size of AC, but running from C to point D.

CD represents the world of thought (*dianoia*), the first of the two intelligible (non-visible realms). But the line does not end there. Imagine, finally, a portion DE, again at the ratio 2:1.

Portion DE of the line represents understanding (*noesis*).

AC is the world of opinion.

AB is imagination (*eikasia*), which deals with conjecture, and BC belief (*pistis*), which deals with our assumptions about visible things.

CE is the realm of knowledge.

CD is thought, which transits the visible and the intelligible. This is the realm of geometry and number, which are abstract, yet count and shape the things of the physical, visible realm. DE, on the other hand, concerns the intelligible alone. This is philosophical understanding, which grasps pure ideas (ideas from "The Good").

The analogy of the divided line overlaps to some extent with the famous Allegory of the Cave.

About the Author

Olavo de Carvalho was born in Campinas, São Paulo State, on April 29, 1947. He has been hailed by the critics as one of the most original and audacious Brazilian thinkers in activity. His work defends human interiority against the tyranny of collective authority, especially when harnessed to a "scientific" ideology. For Olavo de Carvalho, there is an unbreakable link between the objectivity of knowledge and the autonomy of individual consciousness, a bond that gets lost to us when the validity of knowledge is reduced to an impersonal and uniform checklist for use by the academic community.

- t.me/opropriolavo - **Telegram**
- olavodecarvalho.com - **English Site**
- olavodecarvalho.org - **Google Translate**
- seminardefilosofia.org - **Philosophy Seminar***

*The Seminar is, first and foremost, a philosophy course designed to help students practice philosophy rather than simply repeat what others have said about it. The Seminar is also an integral education system open to various fields of knowledge, including literature, the arts, communication and expression, and the natural sciences.

Bibliography

A) Aristotle's works in English translation
The Complete Works of Aristotle. The Revised Oxford Edition, ed. by Jonathan Barnes, 2 vols., Princeton Univ. Press, 1991.

B) Commentaries and Studies
AUBENQUE, Pierre, *La Prudence chez Aristote*, Paris, P.U.F., 1963 (réed. 1993).

AUBENQUE, Pierre, *Le Problème de l'Être chez Aristote. Éssai sur la Problématique Aritotélicienne*, Paris, P.U.F., 1962 (réed. 1991).

BARNES, Jonathan, *Aristóteles*, trad. Martha Sansigre Vidal, Madrid, Cátedra, 1993.

BOUTROUX, Émile, *Études d'Histoire de la Philosophie*, 4e éd., Paris, Alcan, 1925.

BOUTROUX, Émile, *Leçons sur Aristote*, ed. par Jêrome de Grammont, Paris, Éditions Universitaires, 1990.

BRENTANO, Franz, *De la Diversité des Acceptions de l'Être d'après Aristote*, trad. Pascal David, Paris, Vrin, 1992.

Bibliography

COPLESTON, Frederick, *A History of Philosophy*, vol. I, Greece and Rome, New York, Doubleday, 1993.

DUMONT, Jean-Paul, *Introduction à la Méthode d'Aristote*, 2e éd., Paris, Vrin, 1992.

DÜRING, Ingemar, *Aristóteles. Exposición e Interpretación de su Pensamiento*, trad. Bernabé Navarro, México, Universidad Nacional Autónoma, 1990.

GOMEZ-PIN, Víctor, *El Orden Aristotélico*, trad. Virginas Careaga, Barcelona, Ariel, 1984.

HAMELIN, Octave, *Le Système d'Aristote*, éd. Léon Robin, 4e éd., Paris, Vrin, 1985.

JAEGER, Werner, *Aristotle*, Oxford University Press; 2nd Rev Ed, 1962. Trans. Richard Robinson

MANSION, Suzanne, *Études Aristotéliciennes*. Reccueil d'Articles, Louvain-la-Neuve, Institut Supérieur de Philosophie, 1984.

MILLET, Louis, *Aristóteles*, trad. Roberto Leal Ferreira, São Paulo, Martins Fontes, 1990.

MOREAU, Joseph, *Aristote et son École*, Paris, P.U.F., 1962 (réed. 1985).

PORFÍRIO, Isagoge. *Introdução às "Categorias" de Aristóteles*, trad., notas e comentários de Mário Ferreira dos Santos, São Paulo, Matese, 1965.

REALE, Giovanni, *Introducción a Aristóteles*, trad. Victor Bazterrica, Barcelona, Herder, 1985.

ROBIN, Léon, *La Pensée Grecque et les Origines de l'Esprit Scientifique*, Paris, Albin Michel, 1923 (réed. 1973).

ROSS, Sir David, *Aristotle*, Routledge, London & New York; 6th ed (2004)

SPINA, Segismundo, *Introdução à Poética Clássica*, São Paulo, FTD, 1967.

TOMÁS DE AQUINO, Sto., *Comentários a Aristóteles*, trad. Antonio Donato Paulo Rosa, 6 vols., unpublished manuscript.

WEIL, Éric, *Éssais et Conférences*, 2 tomes, Paris, Vrin, 1991.

C) Other works of interest to the study of the Four Discourses

CURTIUS, Ernst-Robert, *European Literature and the Latin Middle Ages*, Harper and Row, 2015.

FEYERABEND, Paul, *Against Method*, London: Verso, 1993.

FRIEDRICH, Hugo, *The Structure of Modern Poetry*, Chap. I. Northwestern University Press; 1st US Edition 1st Printing (January 1, 1974).

FRYE, Northrop, *The Great Code: The Bible and Literature*, Mariner Books, 2002,

HIGHET, Gilbert, *The Classical Tradition. Greek and Roman Influences on Western Literature*, New York, Oxford University Press, 1957.

LAUSBERG, Heinrich, *Handbook of Literary Rhetoric: A Foundation for Literary Study*, trans. David E. Orton, Matthew T. Bliss, R. Dean Anderson, Annemiek Jansen, Brill, 1998.

LE GOFF, Jacques, *Intellectuals in the Middle Ages*, Cambridge: Blackwell Publishers, 1993.

PANOFSKY, Erwin, *Gothic Architecture and Scholasticism*, Cleveland: The World Publishing Company, 1964.

PERELMAN, Chaim, *The New Rhetoric. A Treatise on Argumentation*, Notre Dame: University of Notre Dame Press, 1978.

PRATT, Mary Louise, *Toward a Speech Act Theory of*

Bibliography

Literary Discourse, Bloomington, Indiana University Press, 1977.

SNELL, Bruno, *A Descoberta do Espírito*, trad. Arthur Morão, Lisboa, Edições 70, 1992.

VAN TIEGHEM, Philippe, *Petite Histoire des Grandes Doctrines Littéraires en France. De la Pléiade au Surréalisme*, Paris, P.U.F., 1946.

Notes

Prologue

1. Distributed in handout form to students taking my "Introduction to Intellectual Life" course. As for Chapter II, it is basically the second part of Chapter I of *An Aristotelian Philosophy of Culture*, which I have thought best to split into two here.
2. Sociedade Brasileira para o Progresso de Ciência-SBPC (Brazilian Society for the Advancement of Science) is a nonprofit Organization founded in 1948 to foster scientific, technological, cultural and educational development in Brazil.
3. I'm referring here to the series of articles "Bandidos & Letrados" (Bandits & Intellectuals) that started to appear in *O Jornal do Brasil* as of December 28, 1994.
4. I'm referring here specifically to paragraphs 1, 12 and 13 of the document, which elucidate the scope of my core thesis.
5. e.n. This is a reference to the main character in Mário de Andrade's novel *Macunaíma, o herói sem nenhum caráter* (Macunaíma, the hero without any character), originally published in 1928.

A Preliminary Note to the First Edition of An Aristotelian Philosophy of Culture

1. The present volume goes somewhat further, as Chapter IV lays out one such line of demonstration.
2. *An Aristotelian Philosophy of Culture* contained only chapters I through III.

1. The Four Discourses

1. The two thinkers were Avicenna and St. Thomas Aquinas. In his *Nadjat* (Deliverance), Avicenna (Abu 'Ali el-Hussein ibn Abdallah ibn Sina, 375–428 Hirji/980–1037 CE) firmly asserts the unity of the

four sciences under the general heading of "logic". According to Baron Bernard Carra de Vaux, this "shows how broad his concept of that art is", as he understood it to subsume "the study of the various degrees of persuasion, from rigorous demonstration to poetic suggestion." See *Avicenne* (Paris: Alcan, 1900), 160–161. St. Thomas Aquinas, in I, 1.I, 1–6 of his *Sententia super Posteriora Analytica (Commentary on the Posterior Analytics of Aristotle),* also mentions four degrees of logic (which he likely assimilated from Avicenna). Yet Aquinas regarded those degrees unilaterally on a descending scale, from the most certain (analytical) to the most uncertain (poetic), implying that anything from the *Topics* "down" examined nothing but progressively worse forms of error or, at best, more deficient knowledge. This coincides with neither Avicenna nor with the view I present in this book, and which I believe to be that of Aristotle himself, according to whom there was no real value hierarchy between the discourses, only a difference in function within the four-piece toolkit required to obtain thorough knowledge. One thing we do know is that Thomas Aquinas, like everyone else in the medieval West, had no direct access to Aristotle's *Poetics.* If he had, we can be sure he would never have subscribed to the view that a poetic work was nothing but the rendering of something "pleasant or repulsive" (ibid., no. 6), without meditating more deeply on what Aristotle says about the philosophical value of poetry (*Poetics*, 1451 a). Nevertheless, to have grasped the unity of the four logical sciences with only secondary sources to work from was a truly admirable achievement on Aquinas' part.

2. See Georges Gusdorf, Les Sciences Humaines et la Pensée Occidentale, t. I, *De l'Histoire des Sciences à l'Histoire de la Pensée,* Paris, Payot, 1966 pp. 9-41

3. Reflecting the methodical dualism of his thought, the work of Bachelard can be separated into two blocks: on one hand, there's the series on the philosophy of science, including *Le Nouvel Esprit Scientifique, Le Rationalisme Appliqué,* etc.; and, on the other, those works devoted to the "four elements"—*Le Psychanalyse du Feu, L'Air et les Songes,* etc., in which the rationalist on vacation freely exercises what he called "the right to dream". Bachelard seems to have had a mental railroad switch that allowed him to move between these two worlds without ever incurring the temptation to build a bridge between them.

4. For a critical examination of this theory, see Jerre Levy, "Right Brain, Left Brain: Fact and Fiction" (*Psychology Today*, May 1995, pp. 43 on).

Notes

5. Ezra Pound made a real song and dance about Ernest Fenallosa's essay *The Chinese Written Character as a Medium for Poetry* (London, Stanley Nott, 1936), giving the Western world the impression that the Chinese language constituted a closed world all of its own, ruled by categories of thought inaccessible to Western comprehension other than by subjecting our concept of language to a serious bout of contortion. However, Chinese symbolism is a good deal more similar to its Western counterpart than fans of cultural chasms care to imagine. One clear example of this lies in the similarity that seems to have escaped many between the Chinese *I Ching* and Aristotle's syllogistic logic.

6. A belief in the theory of the two hemispheres is common to all "New Age" theorists and gurus, such as Marilyn Ferguson, Shirley MacLaine, and Fritjof Capra. Concerning the latter, see my book *A Nova Era e a Revolução Cultural. Fritjof Capra & Antonio Gramsci* (The New Age and Cultural Revolution: Fritjof Capra & Antonio Gramsci) [Rio: Instituto de Artes Liberais & Stella Caymmi Editora, 1994]. The funny thing about this theory is that, in trying to overcome Western man's schizophrenia, it starts out by granting it an anatomical foundation (a fictional one, of course). As the rest of this essay will make clear, I don't lend much credence to attempts (as praiseworthy in intent as they are miserable in results) to overcome this dualism by means of a generalized methodological mishmash that acknowledges rhetorical persuasiveness and imaginative effusion as criteria of scientific validity. See, for instance, Paul Feyerabend, *Against Method*, (London: Verso, 1993).

7. "It is perhaps going too far to expect that an author's works should correspond point for point with the classification of the sciences as the author understands it" (Octave Hamelin, Le Système d'Aristotle, published by Léon Robin, 4th ed. Paris. J. Vrin. 1985, p. 82.

8. I'm referring here to the period of "scholastic rhetoric". See Ernst Robert Curtius, *European Literature and the Latin Middle Ages*, Harper and Row, 2015. p.62 ss.

9. This makes the plot of Umberto Eco's *The Name of the Rose* all the funnier, as the uninformed reader might be misled into thinking the story is based on some semblance of historical truth. However, how could a conflict arise over the Second Part of Aristotle's *Poetics* at a time when not even the First was known?

10. Considering its medieval context, the phenomenon I describe certainly bears a relation to a social stratification that put wise men and philosophers (the priestly class) above poets (a class of court servants and fairground performers). The poets' inferior status vis-à-

Notes

vis the sages is conspicuous, both in the social hierarchy (as can be seen in the decisive role in the development of medieval literature played by the *clerici vagantes*, or goliards, a kind of "ecclesiastic proletariat" on the fringe of the universities) and the hierarchy of the sciences themselves: literary studies were rigorously excluded from the scholastic educational system and the highest philosophical conceptions of the Middle Ages were written in the coarsest Latin, though this struck no one as odd at the time, much less incite the kind of aestheticist scandal it later would in the Renaissance. See Jacques Le Goff, *Intellectuals in the Middle Ages*, (Cambridge: Blackwell Publishers, 1993), I § 7.

11. "They're going to demolish the house/but my room will remain intact", lines 8 & 9, "A última canção do beco", Manoel Bandeira (1942).

12. See Werner Jaeger, *Aristotle*, Oxford University Press; 2nd Rev Ed, 1962. Trans. Richard Robinson (German original published in 1923).

13. This finding sparked a dispute among those interpreters who regarded Aristotle as a *systematic* thinker (one who always starts from the same general principles) and those who saw him as an *aporetic* thinker (one who faces problems one by one, moving from the particular toward the general, without any clear idea of where this will lead). Among other things, the approach suggested in the present work aspires to resolve that dispute. See Chap. VII.

14. See Eric Weil, "La place de la logique dans la pensée aristotélicienne (The Place of Logic in Aristotelian Thought)," in Éssais et Conferences (Essays and Conferences), vol.1, Philosophie (Paris: Vrin, 1991), 43–80.

15. Sir David Ross, *Aristotle*, Routledge, London & New York; 6th ed (2004). p. 289.

16. Right from its first annotated translation by Francesco Robortelli in 1548, the *Poetics* would go on to shape literary taste in Europe for the next two and a half centuries, even as Aristotelianism was being banished from the philosophy of nature by the inexorable march of the new science of Galileo, Bacon, Newton, and Descartes. On the one hand, this reveals a complete separation between literary thought and scientific and philosophical development—a separation that is typical of the modern Western world and that has only worsened over the centuries. On the other, it also shows the indifference toward the rediscovered Aristotelian text amongst philosophers. On the Aristotelian roots of the aesthetics of European classicism, see René Wellek, *A History of Modern Criticism: 1750-1950*,

Notes

vol. I, *The Later Eighteenth Century,* (New Haven: Yale University Press, 1955), I, Chap. I.

17. Owing to technical difficulties, I have had to omit the accents on the Greek words.

18. Four aspects of the history of contemporary thought underscore the importance of these observations. I. All attempts to isolate and define a "poetic language" according to its intrinsic characteristics, i.e., to differentiate it materially from "logical" or "everyday language", have failed miserably. On this, see Mary Louise Pratt, *Toward a Speech Act Theory of Literary Discourse* (Bloomington, IN, Indiana University Press, 1977). 2. In the opposite direction, ever since Kurt Gödel, there is general agreement as to the impossibility of erasing every intuitive trace from logical thinking. 3. Chaim Perelman, *The New Rhetoric. A Treatise on Argumentation* (Notre Dame: University of Notre Dame Press, 1978), Thomas S. Kuhn, *The Structure of Scientific Revolutions* (Chicago: University of Chicago, 1996), and Paul Feyerabend, *Against Method* (London: Verso, 1988) all demonstrate the impossibility of entirely expunging the dialectical or even rhetorical from a scientific/analytical proof. 4. At the same time, Erwin Panofsky strongly emphasizes the existence of something that goes beyond mere parallelism between aesthetic (meaning poetic, in the strict sense) and logico-dialectical principles in the medieval vision of the cosmos. See his *Gothic Architecture and Scholasticism*, Erwin Panofsky (Cleveland: The World Publishing Company, 1964). These facts, together with many others pointing in the same direction, indicate that an integrated study of the four discourses is not just expedient, but urgent.

19. Aristotle, *Poetics*, XXV

20. On the three modalities in rhetorical tradition, see Heinrich Lausberg, *Handbook of Literary Rhetoric: A Foundation for Literary Study*, trans. David E. Orton, Matthew T. Bliss, R. Dean Anderson, Annemiek Jansen, Brill, 1998.

21. Aristotle, *Rhetoric,* 1358a-1360a.

22. Aristotle, *Topics, VIII,* 14

23. The difference between analytics and dialectics "is, according to Aristotle, that which exists between a course taught by a teacher and a discussion among peers—in other words, the difference between scientific monologue and scientific dialogue." Eric Weil, "La Place de la Logique dans la Pensée Aristotélicienne" (The Place of Logic in Aristotelian Thought), 64.

24. It is practically impossible that Aristotle, a natural scientist with a mind full of analogies between the sphere of rational concepts and

facts of a physical order, would fail to note the parallel—direct and inverse—between the four discourses and the four elements, themselves arranged upon a concentric scale that goes from the densest to the subtlest. In a course I delivered at the IAL in 1988 (unpublished other than in a series of hand-outs under the general title "Theory of the Four Discourses", I investigated this parallel more thoroughly. Here, however, it suffices to mention it in passing.

25. Understood as the first operation of the intellect and so the basis for all further reasoning.

26. See Pierre Aubenque, Pierre Aubenque, *Le probleme de l'etre chez Aristote* Paris: Presses Universitaires de France, 1962

2. An Aristotelian Model of Cultural History

1. Northrop Frye, *The Great Code: The Bible and Literature*, Mariner Books, 2002, p.6

2. Cf. Eduard Zeller, *Outlines of the History of Greek Philosophy*, ed. Wilhelm Nestle, trans. by L. R, Palmer. New York, Meridian Books, 1955. Pp. 24-36 (The German original dates to 1883, and is a summary the author made of his own monumental work *Philosophie Der Griechen*)

3. On scholastic rhetoric, see Ernst-Robert Curtius, *European Literature and the Latin Middle Ages*, Harper and Row, 2015. Chapter IV, 4 & 8.

4. On the dialectic in German idealism, see Josiah Royce's ever-pertinent *Lectures on Modern Idealism*, 1906.

5. See José Ortega y Gasset, La Idea de Principio en Leibniz y la Evolución de la Teoría Deductiva, em Obras Completas, Madrid, Alianza Editorial, 1983, t. 8.

6. This does not mean to say that the argument's public credibility derives from the fact that it really has any scientific (logico-analytical) basis, merely that the public assumes that it does. Likewise, the mythopoetic discourse, during its heyday, did not necessarily possess all the properties Frye attributed to it, it just had to be seen to possess them. Today, anti-smoking legislation or anti-inflation decrees are not accepted because they are based on unquestionable scientific validity (something we could debate almost indefinitely), but because the wider public believes that they are. Similarly, the Shaman's authority did not derive from his factually possessing magical powers, but from the general belief that he did. In all these cases, the ground for credibility is a little like the self-fulfilling

Notes

prophecy: if society believes an idea is scientifically grounded, it will pump research funding in that direction, to the detriment of other areas of investigation. As Levi-Strauss so clearly saw, widespread belief in a magical power is, to a certain point at least, the source of actual magical power (see "The Sorcerer and his Magic", 1963. In *Structural Anthropology*. Pp. 167-85. New York: Basic Books.)

7. Curtius, op. cit., Chap. I, sees in this phenomenon the origin of the peculiarities that distinguish European literature from all others.

8. A very current theme, in Brazil at least, where the dispute between social democrats and neoliberals pits dialectic against analytical logic. Elucidating the differences between methodological precepts is the only way I can see to arbitrate in this debate with any fairness, as I tried to do myself in the closing pages of *O Jardim das Aflições* (*The Garden of Afflictions*). Needless to say, authority does not imply validity in either case, merely the supposition of validity; social democratic dialectic and neoliberal logic does not always go beyond mere rhetorical allegation.

9. See Hugo Friedrich, *The Structure of Modern Poetry*, Chap. I. Northwestern University Press; 1st US Edition 1st Printing (January 1, 1974)

10. Muslim rhetoric reached the height of perfection with the first generation after the Prophet, with Imam Ali.

11. As occurs, for example, in F. Capra *The Turning Point*, Bantam; Reissue edition (August 1, 1984).

3. The Presence of Aristotelian Discourse in Western History

1. A lecture given at the Permanent Seminar on Philosophy and the Humanities at the *Instituto de Artes Liberais*, in May 1992. Recorded and transcribed by students and corrected by the author.

2. The pedagogical applications of the Theory of the Four Discourses will not be dealt with in the present volume. They are not so much a project as a work underway for over almost a decade now at the *Seminário de Filosofia*.

3. *Metaphysics*, A, 1. 980a 21-30

4. Benedetto Croce, *Logica come Scienza del Concetto Puro*, Bari, Laterza, 1971 [1st ed. 1905] p.5.

5. Cf. Maurice Pradines, *Traite de Psychologie Générale*, v. I, *Le Psychisme Elémentaire*, 3rd ed. P.U.F. 1948, pp. 108-109; 376-379; 390-396 & 691-726.

6. See Jean Piaget, *Biologie et Connaissance*, Paris, Gallimard, 1967.

Notes

7. It is also in this deep sense, and not just as a student of comparative anatomy, that Charles Darwin considered Aristotle to be a precursor to evolutionary theory. However, when we see that Aristotelian evolutionism is shaped along the lines of potency and act, it becomes even more plausible to also look to Aristotle for a principle with which to arbitrate between and reconcile evolutionary and anti-evolutionary theories through the use of a dialectic that distinguishes between the various acceptations of the concepts. For a long time, there was perceived to be an intrinsic incompatibility between the concepts of fixed species and animal evolution; but I believe this incompatibility is overcome through a simple distinction between logical (metaphysical) and biological species—a distinction that would certainly not have escaped Aristotle himself, who so often stressed the non-existence of pure logico-mathematical forms in nature.

8. Entelechy, Greek *entelecheia*, is "that which realizes or makes actual what is otherwise merely potential" (Encyclopedia Britannica). —E.N.

9. Cf. Karl Marx, *1st Thesis on Feuerbach*.

10. Pradines, op. cit.

11. See Erwin Panofsky, *Architecture Gothique et Pensée Scolastique*, trans. Pierre Bourdieu, Paris, Les Éditions de Minuit, 1978.

12. Segismundo Spina, *Introdução à Poética Clássica*, São Paulo, F.T.D., 1967, p.47

13. Spina, op. cit.

14. See Edgar de Bruyne, *The Aesthetics of the Middle Ages*, Frederick Ungar Pub. Co, 1969.

15. In the Middle Ages, the "classical education" taught the seven liberal arts. These were divided into two groups, the Trivium (Threefold), which consisted of logic, rhetoric and grammar, and the Quadrivium (Fourfold), which encompassed arithmetic, music, geometry and astronomy. — E.N.

16. See Umberto Eco, *Il Problema Estetico in Tommaso d'Aquino*, 2nd ed. Milan, Bompiani, 1970.

17. See Gilbert Durand, *Science de l'Homme et Tradition*, Paris, Tête-de-Feuilles/Sirac, 1978.

18. Saint Thomas mentions scales of credibility but taken in the sense of a scale of validity, which would mean judging the Four Discourses from an analytical perspective, as a model for perfection toward which the other discourses were building. Basically, Saint Thomas brushed against the subject, but never broached it directly.

4. The Universal Typology of the Discourses

1. Lecture recorded on tape and transcribed by Ana Célia Rodrigues. São Paulo, 1989. Distributed to the author's students as a handout in January 1991.

2. The same goes for narratives: every narrative can, in principle, go deeper and deeper into the past or press indefinitely into the future.

5. The Conditions of Credibility

1. Ceci (Cecilia) and Peri were the unlikely lovers in José de Alencar's 1857 novel *O Guarani*. Peri was a Guarani Indian warrior who fell in love with Cecília, the daughter of a Portuguese nobleman. Ceci and Peri feature, among other Alencar characters, on a monument to the author in Rio de Janeiro.

2. Baron of Itararé, pseudonym of the writer, journalist and political humorist Aparício Fernando de Brinkerhoff Torelly, aka Apporelly, who frequently satirized the Integralists.

3. *Opera omnia XVI/1*, p. 103

6. Milestones in the History of Aristotelian Studies in the West

1. See René Wellek, *History of Modern Criticism: 1750-1950: The Late Nineteenth Century: 004*, Yale University Press, 1965, Chapters 1 to 7; Philippe Van Tiegham, *Petite Histoire des Grandes Doctrines Littéraires en France, De la Pléiade au Surréalisme*, Paris, P.U.F., 1946, pp 1-58; Paul Hazard, *The Crisis of the European Mind, 1680-1715*, trans J. Lewis May, New York Review of Books, 2013, Chapters 1-2.

2. Of course, there are other interesting developments in the history of Aristotelian studies, some of which are quite recent, but they do not add much to the themes at hand. See, for example, M. A. Sinceur [org.], *Aristote Aujourd'hui, Études Réunes à l'Occasion du 2,300e Anniversaire da la Morte du Philosophe*, Paris, Ères, 1988. Others fall within the scope of our interest, but neither buttress nor detract from our thesis. I'm referring here to David Metzger, *The Lost Cause of Rhetoric. The Relation of Rhetoric and Geometry in Aristotle and Lacan*, Carbondale and Edwardsville, Southern Illinois University Press,

Notes

1995, and to Victor Gomez-Pin, *El Orden Aristotélico*, Barcelona, Ariel, 1984. The recent wave of debates in the English-speaking world have concentrated, on the one hand, on interpretations of *De Anima* to ascertain whether or not Aristotelian psychobiology can be considered a precursor to present-day materialist functionalism (See Martha Nussbaum and Amélie Oksenberg Rorty, *Essays on Aristotle's De Anima*, Oxford, Clarendon, 1995); and, on the other, the question of ethics (See Anthony Kenny, *Aristotle on the Perfect Life*, Oxford, Clarendon, 1995). Neither theme is particularly relevant to the thesis being developed here.

3. Jean-Paul Dumont, *Introduction à la Méthode d'Aristote*, 2nd edition, Paris, Vrin, 1992, p. 208. Author's translation and italics.

4. Edgar Morin, *La Métode. I. La Nature de la Nature*, Le Seuil, 1977, p. 9. Author's translation.

7. Notes on a Possible Conclusion

1. [E.N.] *Modus exponendi et argumentandi*, proceeding by method of exposition and argument.

2. It seems the first to float this hypothesis was Rudolf Carnap. To disprove it one need only note that the first grammatical speculations in Greece date to two centuries after Aristotle.

3. Jonathan Barnes, *Aristotle, a Very Short Introduction*, Oxford University Press, 1982, reissued 1996, p. 66.

4. See Dumont, *op. cit.*

5. See Franz Brentano, *On the Several Senses of Being in Aristotle,* University of California Press (1976). First published in 1862.

6. *Rep.* 509d6 to 511e5

7. The theme of apodeictic science as a normative ideal would be taken up anew over two millennia later by Edmund Husserl in his *The Crisis of European Sciences and Transcendental Phenomenology*. Husserl saw a return to this ideal as the sole hope of salvation for European society in the face of imminent catastrophe. The present work is openly inspired by Husserl's program (see *The Crisis of European Sciences and Transcendental Phenomenology*, trans. David Carr, Northwestern University Press, 1970).

Notes

I. De re Aristotelica Opiniones Abominandae: The Dead Cat's Meow

1. The reasons for this are explained further on, in § 17.

2. The consultant complains of the "paucity of the bibliography presented", but as it contains works by Jaeger, Weil, Hamelin, Ross and Zeller, all classics in Aristotelian studies, I can only assume they mean quantitative paucity. Can it be this person actually reads *Ciência Hoje*? If they did, they would see that twenty-five titles is the average bibliography presented in published papers. To surpass that number would—beyond incurring the risk of endless and unnecessary quotations—be rather bad form.

3. *Peri Herm.*, 4: l7a.

4. See, for example, Jean-Paul Dumont, Introduction à la Méthode d'Aristote, 2e. Éd. révue et augmentée, Paris, Vrin, 1992.

5. Of course, there is nothing in Patristic times that comes even close to the Aristotelian exegeses of the 13th Century in terms of depth and amplitude. But, there is a big difference between saying that this primitive Aristotelianism was of low quality and stating that it never existed at all—about the same difference as saying the SBPC assessment is trash and that the SBPC made no assessment whatsoever.

6. See Uma Filosofia Aristotélica da Cultura. Introdução à Teoria dos Quatro Discursos (Rio de Janeiro, IAL/Caymmi, 1994), p. 16.

7. op., I, 2, 101a-b.

8. *Stromata* A, VI, 33,2

9. Éric Weil *"La place de la logique dans la pensée aristotélicienne"*, em *Éssais et Conférences, vol. I, Paris, Vrin, 1991, p. 64 (cit. na n. 20 de Filosofia Aristotélica da Cultura).*

10. *Poet.*, 1451a

11. Id. Ibid.

12. *Hamlet*, Act II, scene 2. The full line is "What's Hecuba to him, or he to Hecuba, / That he should weep for her?"

13. Allow me to remind the zealous theorizer of Greek theater that I am the author of three short books on the theme of poetics: O Crime da Madre Agnes ou a Confusão entre Espiritualidade e Psiquismo (São Paulo, Speculum, 1983), Símbolos e Mitos no Filme "O Silêncio dos Inocentes" (Rio de Janeiro, IAL/Caymmi, 1992) and Os Gêneros Literários: Seus Fundamentos Metafísicos (Rio de Janeiro, IAL/Caymmi, 1993).

14. *De cælo*, I, 7, 275b.

15. *De gener. anim.*, I, I, 715b.

16. *Met.*, L. 7,1072a. [E.N.] The self-causing cause from which all other beings derive.
17. *Phys.*, IV, 219a-223a.
18. Consigning all Greeks to the cage of eternal return was a demential generalization of Nietzsche's, made to lend an idea of his own invention the aura of classical Greek prestige. When it came to classical philology, the great philosopher-poet was nothing more than a rank amateur whose interpretations, which lacked sufficient textual foundations, were demolished entirely by the analyses of Ulrich von Willamowitz-Möllendorf. I don't know who the consultant had as teachers at university, but it is highly possible, Brazil being Brazil, that there are still academics out there who take Nietzsche seriously as a philologist.
19. *The Four Discourses*, Chapter II, An Aristotelian Model of Culture, section 4.
20. Auguste Comte (1798-1857) held that society as a whole, plus the sciences individually, cycles through three main stages: the theological, the metaphysical, and the positive.
21. Antonio Machado (1875-1939), "On the Banks of the Duero".
22. A reference to the short story by Lima Barreto, 'The Man Who Spoke Javanese", about a conman who makes a successful career pretending to be an expert in Javanese and gets away with it because no-one else knows enough about the language to see through his ruse.
23. Politicians embroiled in major corruption scandals in Brazil around the time this letter was written.

II. Challenge to the Usurpers behind Closed Ranks

1. Published in *O Globo*, Jan. 7, 1995.
2. I'm referring here to the article "Bandidos & Letrados"—*Jornal do Brasil*, December 1994—which, investigating the psychological complicity between Brazilian intellectuals and the gangsters of Rio, drew reactions one could only describe as rabid from certain members of the intellectual community, including Mr. Antônio Callado. The furor around "Bandidos & Letrados" occurred in parallel with the SBPC debacle, but I won't go into it here, because it is not pertinent to the theme of this piece. Some details are given in an appendix to the series of articles reproduced in my book *O Imbecil Coletivo: Atualidades Inculturais Brasileiras* (Rio de Janeiro,

Notes

Faculdade da Cidade Editora and the Brazilian Academy of Philosophy, 1996).

III. Letters to Ênio Candotti

1. I'm referring here to *De Re Aristotelica Opiniones Abominandae*.
2. See letter 1 above
3. As a professional journalist with thirty years' experience, I have always wanted to see scientific debates play out in the pages of the daily broadsheets. I have edited scientific journals myself (*Atualidades Médicas* and *Clínica Geral*), and even then I used to lament that such important subjects were being discussed so far from the eyes of the general public.

Index

Index

Index

brain, hemispheres of, 15
Brazil's role in the spiritual history of the world, 5
Brazilian Philosophy Conference, Fifth, 6
Brecht, Bertolt, 71–72, 119
Brentano, Franz, 82, 113
Brito, Daniel Brilhante de, 7
Brunschvicq, Léon, 128
Bukhari, 36

C
Callado, Antônio, 6, 134
Candotti, Ênio, 2, 132–134, 136–141
Cartesianism, 85
categories, system of, 92
catharsis, 117–119
Catholic dogma, 70
Catholic theology, 32–33
Catholic University of Salvador, state of Bahia, 6
cats, dead and alive, 104–106, 111
Cause, First, 121–123
Cave, Plato's allegorical, 143–145
certainty, desire for maximum, 63–64
China as cultural model, 37
Chomsky, Noam, 46
Christian doctrine, 125
Christianity
    found a master of choice in Aristotle, 97
    Oriental origins of, 32
    preaching of, 8
Cicero, 34

Index

E

F

Farias, P.C., 131

Firmicius Maternus, 113

first philosophy, 106–107

form and matter, 46–47

formal unity, 57

Forms, Plato's theory of, 87, 94–96

Four Discourses, Theory of the, 13–29

   and Plato's Divided Line, 93–97

   and the cognitive process, 27–28

   as beginning and end of Aristotelian philosophy, 28–29

   as concentric circles, 27

   development by author, 11–12

   discourses distinguishable, but not separable, 23–24, 28

   distinguished by level of credibility, 20–24

   historical/philological investigation of, 14, 128

   logical necessity of, deriving, 56–66

   not expounded in any of Aristotle's works, 89

   philosophical critique of, 14

   succession of dominant discourses, 30–37, 125–126

   typology of, aprioristicallly derived, 59–60

foxes and chicken coops, 3

free will, the listener's, in rhetoric, 76

Freud, Sigmund, 69

Frye, Northrop, 75

G

Galeffi, Dante Augusto, 6

Galeffi, Romano, 6

Galileo, 52

genera, 'species of species,' 43, 86

Index

Newton, Isaac, 52
Nicomachus (Aristotle's father), 92
Nietzsche, Friedrich, 130
Nóbrega, Fr. Manoel da, 8
noesis, 'understanding,' 94–96, 144
noeta, 'the intelligible world,' 94
Nunes, Rosângela, 135

O

odontology, 102, 138–139
Oedipus complex, 69
Oedipus Rex (Sophocles), 69
On the Several Senses of Being in Aristotle (Brentano), 82
oracles, Greek, 30
organic development, in the history of philosophy, 40-41, 91
Origen, 125
Orsini, Elizabeth, 7

P

paradox of the image, 44–45
patristic period, 32, 111, 113, 124, 163
peirastic and other 'trial' words in *peir-* and *pir-,* 22
peitho, 'persuasion,' 21
Peri and Ceci (statues), 70
permanence through change, 36
phantasia, 'memory, imagination,' 27, 42, 86
phantasma, 'image,' 42, 86
phenomenology, 68
philology, necessary to understand most poetic works, 68–71

Index

Printed in Great Britain
by Amazon